Sense & Sensibilily is a _ _____ *Nest project*
Presented at _____ *Onomatopee, Eindhoven*
From _____ *September 2017 to March 2018*
Curated by _____ *Pernilla Ellens*
Introducing the works of 6 visual makers:
_____ *Mandy Roos*
Gabriel A. Maher in collaboration with
Roberto Pérez Gayo & Carly Rose Bedford
_____ *Olle Lundin*
_____ *Janina Frye*

Sense & Sensibility — September 17– March 18

3

Table of contents

Sense & Sensibility — 5
Editor's introduction:
Sense & Sensibility: what a girl wants, what a girl needs — 7
The Girls' Room: a perfect hideaway to dream away — 13

Mandy Roos — 17
The Girls' Room
Introducing *The Girls' Room* — 18
About the show and Mandy Roos — 33
Inside the *The Girls' Room* — 35
Mermaids leather & drink-straw dresses — 41
— Pernilla Ellens

Gabriel A. Maher, Roberto Pérez Gayo, — 49
& Carly Rose Bedford
" _____ "
Introducing "_____" — 50
About the show and Gabriel A. Maher, — 65
Roberto Pérez Gayo and Carly Rose Bedford
Methodological considerations — 69
— Gabriel A. Maher, Roberto Pérez Gayo
and Carly Rose Bedford

Olle Lundin — 81
Bureau Just: Agency for Feminist Practices
Introducing *Bureau Just: Agency for Feminist Practices* — 82
About the show and Olle Lundin — 97
Letter to Olle — 99
— Charlotte van Buylaere
Selected questions and answers — 106
Justify my love! Interview with Olle Lundin — 108
— Charlotte van Buylaere and Pernilla Ellens

Table of contents

Janina Frye
People are nowhere near so fluid — 113

Introducing *People are nowhere near so fluid* — 114
About the show and Janina Frye — 129
More or less (than) human: on objects in the practice of Janina Frye — 131
— Alicja Melzacka

More girlfriends! — 145
Curator's note — 147
Daantje Bons — 148
Camille Auer — 152
Nasty Women — 156

Theoretical girls — 159
Curator's note — 161
Blinded by Fashion – why feminism on a t-shirt is oppression dressed up as politics — 163
— Aynouk Tan
The Politics of Pitch — 167
— Nina Power [contextual reflection on the work of Maher, Gayo and Bedford] — 175
Design and Intersectionality: Material Production of Gender, Race, Class — and Beyond — 183
— Ece Canlı, Luiza Prado de O. Martins
Material Thinking and the Agency of Matter
— Barbara Bolt

Colophon — 190
Boy bye! — 191

Sense & Sensibility September 17– March 18

5

Pernilla Ellens

Sense & Sensibility: what a girl wants, what a girl needs

Sense & Sensibility gives a place to explore contrasts and oppositions between gender constructs, objects and subjects, and between theories and visual modes of culture. Onomatopee, as a platform, has a signalling function: it spots a trend in contemporary culture, and instead of making a statement, it asks questions about the reality of the trend and practice itself. The trend we're now talking about is feminism as a fashionable commodity in today's capitalist culture. Inclusive gender liberation goes way beyond the commodification of the colour pink, the repetition of feminist slogans on cheap tshirts and the popularisation of genderneutralism. Onomatopee dissects the trend by giving four local artists and makers the chance to reflect upon the topic of gender in their own way; so, instead of proposing new exclusive statements, we open up for otherness and inclusiveness. Sense & Sensibility gives space for a more inclusive and varied reflection on contemporary feminism and the role of gender in politics, society and philosophy. In this way we can contribute to discourse without claiming authority or

Sense & Sensibility: what a girl wants, what a girl needs

wholeness, and will also avoid contributing to the commodification of the topic.

The Young Girl

Started during September 2017, Sense & Sensibility exists as a group show, as well as in solo presentations, performances and this publication. For one month (or a bit more) each local artist had space at Onomatopee to research, show, tell, intervene, perform, express and explore their relationship to the theme, often in cooperation with others. The projects take feminism and girlhood as starting points for various reflections and expressions; they go beyond defining a social movement or theoretical constructs. Or, as trans zine maker Camille Auer puts it: "I think it's instrumental to have a wide understanding of girlhood when promoting girl power. Otherwise it will fall into the category of cissupremacy instead of the intended gender liberation." A pivotal literary work of the project is Tiqqun's Preliminary Materials For a Theory of a Young Girl (Semiotext(e), 1999). In that it's stated: "The Young-Girl is not always young; more and more frequently, she is not even female. She is the figure of total integration in a disintegrating social totality." The Young-Girl is the ultimate product of the consumer society, the model citizen of capitalism; she can only seduce by consuming. In this book, the Young-Girl seeks her own reflection

Pernilla Ellens

in corporate universals. Consumer society is colonising sexuality and conceals this process as 'freedom.' The Young-Girl can do what she wants with her body, as long as it's part of the capitalist process in which the Young-Girl and her ideals are for sale in the marketplace. It is precisely this process that is currently unfolding in our culture. Onomatopee is signalling that it wishes to rebel against it, not by creating a perfect alternative, ready to be sold again, but by showing a variety of voices and processes, and by embracing diversity in discourse about feminism and gender. Throughout the project and in this book, we use the language of marketing (like a Situationist detournement technique) to emphasize the capitalist structures girls, women and other non-cis-male identities are living in, conditioned by words as expressed specifically in song lyrics and in magazine slogans.

Dream baby dream

We try to make sense of realities by getting together during changing situations, rather than by defining a status quo. We try to be sensible, by embracing diversity within the interpretation of the theme. Sense & Sensibility goes beyond defining a social movement and theoretical constructs, it takes feminism as a starting point for various reflections and expressions around inequality. From our starting point, the teenage girl, we learned to open

Sense & Sensibility: what a girl wants, what a girl needs

up to intersectional frameworks. Feminism is not about the emancipation of women only, or simply about trying to eliminate the differences between women and men on social, political and economic levels; these goals are wonderful, but are also very limited to white privileged cis-gender women. Instead, contemporary feminism should lay bare power structures and speak for all minorities that are victimised by the patriarchy. In subsequent projects, the participants asked questions to us, the audience in Eindhoven and beyond about contemporary girlhood, the feminist voice, equality on the street and the relations between objects and subjects. We, as Onomatopee, learned from all participants and were in constant dialogue with them and the audience. Starting out as a platform for four local artists to think about inequality, between two gender constructs, between objects and subjects and between theories and visual modes of culture, the project is now the starting point for further discussion about what feminism can do within the institution and how we can give space to voices without capitalising them.

What a girl wants, what a girl needs

Growing up isn't easy, and so we, as Onomatopee, felt the need to provide a platform where girlhood, contemporary feminism, thoughts on gender and equality and the dif

Pernilla Ellens

ferences between objects and subjects can be researched and discussed as freely as possible. Within The Girls' Room we respond to the current gender liberation trend by offering both theory and praxis through engaged artists working within the wider theme. In stylistic phenomena and aesthetics, Onomatopee's Girls' Room is referring to the 90s American highschool teen bedroom, and therefore is a literal nod to the capitalist trend that is being mistaken for contemporary feminism. Within and around the bedroom designed by Mandy Roos, there are contributions by all participants from the Nest 2017 project and from others willing to engage. The Girls' Room functions as a reading room, a workshop, an exhibition hall and as a space where dialogue between visitors and the project's participants can take place.

Want to visit The Girls' Room yourself?
Just go the next pages to find out more! ❤

...sibility

...ace; a safe space,
...ages and teenage
...one and read,
...ore her body and
...pillows. In her own
...reely about who
... becoming – all the
...e dangerous
...n however is not
...a physical space
...ory and praxis
...od, gender, bodies
...om, a meeting
...onstantly changing
...d by Mandy Roos,
...riety of her tactile
...s by Olle Lundin,
...e and others willing
...etypical teenage
...ct, we open up
...a girl and who's not
...e and biological
...ctured and shaped

The Girls' Room

September
October
November
December

Pernilla Ellens

The Girls' Room: a perfect hideaway to dream away

A girls' room is a magical place: a safe space, constructed from cinematic images and teenage dreams. Here, a girl can be alone. She can read, dance, pose in front of the mirror, get dressed, explore her body and hide away. In her own room, a girl can think and act freely about who she is and discover who she is becoming, all while being pressured by the dangers of the outside world. Girls who want so many things, but are constricted by the pressures of authorities, can create their own identity within these 15 square meters. Surrounded by her favourite books, records, colours and cushions, the girls' room is the perfect hideaway to dream away.

Bring it on (2000)

In contrast to this personal safe space, there is the brutally dangerous outside world. Here girls are catcalled, molested and attacked.

14 The Girls' Room: a perfect hideaway to dream away

They have less access to education, a harder time finding a job, and earn less than guys. Girls feel the hot breath of their parents and their societal surroundings to succeed both professionally and personally. They should get married to the right man and start a family, all

But I'm a cheerleader (1999)

Hairspray (1962)

while looking gorgeous and staying healthy. Girls must always suppress their sexuality in order to not get raped, and so often disappoint themselves in their search for identity. As a girl leaving your teen room, health care bills now fall on your doormat. Being a girl suddenly doesn't have so much to do with curling your hair in front of the fairy-light lit mirror, but more with trying to keep your reproductive organs vital and your head clear, so you're able to perform at your best during university and work. Your self

Pernilla Ellens

esteem has to be as hard as rock if you are to make it through the day whilst being treated like an excess, a waste of space, an object for others to use or a troublemaker.

<u>*You've been a very bad girl.*</u>
<u>*Now go to your room!*</u>

The Girls' Room, as it appeared at Onomatopee, is a concept for exploring gender trouble and expressing identity. The lush pink space, where a girl can act and think freely, explore her sexuality and where her identity can take shape, is in dazzling contrast to the current political climate, where LGBTQA protesters are being arrested and a violent cis-male supremacy is reigning the world.

Mandy and Pernilla during the opening of The Girls' Room

The Girls' Room functions as a safe space where contributing artists can express their position toward gender trouble, even though outside of this space it's very hard to effect real change within the current political state of affairs. This is especially true when, as we speak, women's health organisations are being dismantled and violence against those who

The Girls' Room: a perfect hideaway to dream away

identify as something other than heterosexual is increasingly pertinent. Moreover, The Girls' Room conceals societal standards about what defines a girl, where her place in the world is, and what she should do with her body. It is a place that is constructed from images and dreams, but also where identities take shape.

Visitor reading in The Girls' Room library

Olle Lundin interviewing Freek Lomme for Bureau Just about feminism

It is the place where girls can be alone and write in their diaries, look in the mirror and shape their own image. They can listen to their favourite punk bands and find a way to rebel and express themselves within this little private space. However, this doesn't decrease the pressure from outside. The Girls' Room is the space where the future is being dreamed up, where one can reflect on memories from the past and where contemporary struggles are taking place.

Mandy Roos — The Girls' Room

Sense & Sensibility nº1 — September 17

Softie Mandy

Introduction

The Girls' Room

2 September 2017 – 11 March 2018

The Girls' Room at Onomatopee is not only created by or for girls. It is a physical space and a starting point for both theory and praxis regarding contemporary girlhood, gender, bodies and identities. It is a reading room, a meeting place, a group exhibition and a constantly changing installation, all in one. Designed by Mandy Roos, the Girls' Room features a variety of her tactile textile pieces, and includes contributions by Olle Lundin, Gabriel A. Maher, Janina Frye, Daantje Bons, Camille Auer and Barbara Smith, who represents Nasty Women. By making the archetypical teenage girl the protagonist of the project, we open up the conversation about who's a girl and who's not, in terms of bodies, performance and biological identity. Furthermore, we can question who her friends are and what kind of shapes, materials and colours she surrounds herself with. What books does she read? What records does she listen to? How does she explore sexuality? How does she deal with issues of femininity, such as body hair? In a playful manner, via her interior design and via her autonomous work, Mandy Roos has hidden all the answers to these questions in The Girls' Room.

About Mandy Roos

Mandy Roos (1987, NL)

Mandy Roos graduated from Design Academy Eindhoven in 2014, direction Man and Identity. After being active for the Textielmuseum Tilburg, she now works a freelance fashion designer and interior stylist who also specialises in textile practices. Roos plays with the expectations of typical objects and unexpected materials, and the work produced covers both domestic and haute couture. She makes interior objects, shoes, masks, underwear and other forms of fashion, and has documented her own style in various inspiration books for the shoe industry. Some of her projects where she researches the potency of material, form and function, are *Softie Wanted*, *Chaussures de Fleures* en *Invasion of the Foot Carrier*. At first glance, the work of Roos seems cheeky and incites you to touch, play and feel the various fabrics and materials. But upon closer inspection, the decorative objects and wearable interior applications tickle you to think about the relationship between object and subject, material and function.

Works displayed in *The Girls' Room*

Mandy Roos & Victoria Ledig
Softie Wanted (2017)

For The Girls' Room, Mandy Roos expanded her collection Softie Wanted with two new rugs: the bold blue/purple gradient one placed in the middle of the space, and the textured round magenta one, lying relaxed in the corner. The rugs could function as interior applications, but could also be playful sculptures. The creation of both the blue-purple rectangular shaped rug, and the pink lip-shaped pink rug with nipple effect were commissioned by Onomatopee.

Mandy Roos
Trichophilia (2017)

Trichophilia is a series of undergarments that refer to hair fetishism. For The Girls' Room, Mandy created a new and unique kind of hand-made panties. Glittery and gradient embroidery makes them look as if they're full of lush pubic hair. With this collection, Mandy attempts to celebrate (female) body hair, instead of despising it. By using catchy colours and crafty techniques to re-create pubic hair, Mandy has created something beautiful for a natural quality that is often perceived as ugly; which thereby helps to break the taboo around body hair.

Works displayed in The Girls' Room

Mandy Roos & Victoria Ledig
Softie Wanted (2016)

"Fresh industrial foam seeks young, bold interior application. To fool around, long term commitment possible. Good looks, sense of humour and love for cuddles are a must. In search of the humour and inner nature of materials - the industrial, profane and the fanciful meet up. Creating tangible imagery rooted in play and experimentation."

Mandy Roos & Victoria Ledig
Softie Wanted More (2016)

Softie Wanted More is a wearable interior application. It's a dress, a sculpture, a wall hanging and a thing to marvel at all-in one. Made from drinking straws in the typically gender-normed colours, *Softie Wanted More* changes shape in every new position and context. Besides its function as an interior design, the piece has also been shown as haute couture at international fashion shows like *Fashion Clash*. You can see the model, wearing the dress on the little photo on the desk. The shoes that are also exhibited in The Girls' Room are designed by Chris van den Elzen and were created especially for the object.

Works displayed in *The Girls' Room*

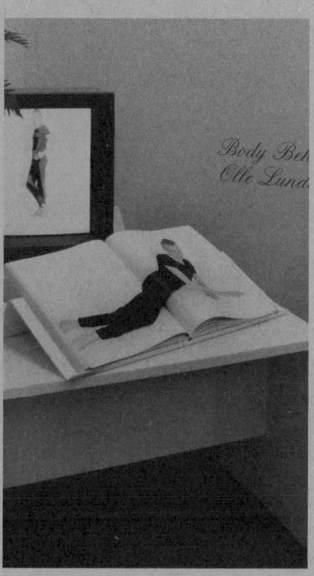

Gabriel A. Maher
Instruction 01/Garment (2015)

Instruction 01 is a performative and behavioural tool designed to articulate, define and reconfigure ideas about the construction of gender. In this work, a set of instructions activate a sequence of movements through the act of sitting. These instructions take the form of a graphic code and explore the position itself, the space taken up by the position, the garment which articulates the position and the site of the body. *Instruction 01* considers what it means to take a position, and investigates how clothing establishes order and directs our behaviour in ways that have been layered with gendered meaning - the body is formulated as a consequence.

Olle Lundin
Body Behaviour (2006-2015)

Posing for 13 hours straight and taking on 4000 poses, Olle tried to recreate each pose that was shown in every Vogue March edition between 2006 and 2015. In order to understand how to move his body in three dimensions, Olle worked with the choreographer and designer Sara Kaiser. In the book and video *Body Behaviour*, Olle tries to re-enact female postures with the male body. Which postures are you allowed to take as a man or woman? How are you being read? Questions concerning identity are then raised. In the book, the poses are photographed chronologically. *Body Behaviour* is exploring gendered performativity through a playful criticality of mass media culture and high fashion advertising.

Works displayed in The Girls' Room

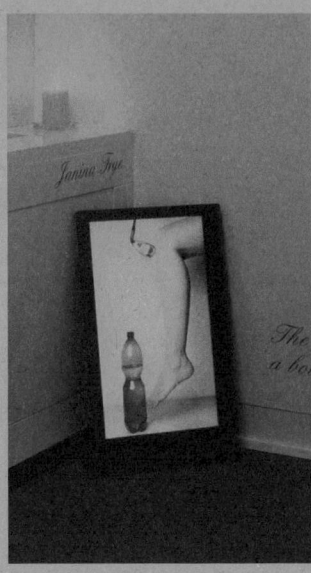

Janina Frye
The innocence of a golf club, a leg and a bottle,
[Communication with the Non-Human] (2016)

For this video, Janina was figuring out ways to communicate with objects. In order to communicate with an object, the human has to be on the same level as the object itself. As objects are always innocent, or so Janina states, she had to find a way where the human, or at least a part of the human is innocent too. In doing so, she decided to work with the reflexes of the human body, as they're not controlled by a conscious line of thought.

Pre-reflexive : Descriptive of an individual's immediate, uncritical reaction to something prior to any conscious evaluation. For example, when someone knows that they enjoyed a film without knowing why. Compare reflexivity. For Sartre, a state of consciousness prior to reflection that he tries to reconstruct as part of his argument that personal consciousness depends on reflection.

Source: oxfordreference.com

The Girls' Room's Library

PUBLICATIONS

Kathy Acker, McKenzie Wark, *I'm very into you: Correspondence 1995-1996* (2015), Autonomedia.

Judith Butler, *Gender Trouble: feminism and the subversion of identity* (1990), Taylor & Francis Ltd.

Sheila Jeffreys, *Beauty and Misogyny: Harmful cultural practices in the west* (2014), Taylor & Francis Ltd.

Sarah Marcus, *Girls to the Front* (2010), HarperCollins Publishers Inc.

Laurie Penny, *Unspeakable Things* (2014), Bloomsbury.

Meike Schalk, Thérèse Kristiansson, and Ramia Mazé, *Feminist Futures of Spatial Practice* (2017), Spurbuchverlag.

Valerie Solanas, *Scum Manifesto* (1968), Verso Books.

Tiqqun, *Preliminary Materials For a Theory of the Young-Girl* (1999), semiotext(e).

Andy Zeisler, *We Were Feminists Once* (2016), Ingram Publisher Services US.

RECORDS

G.L.O.S.S. – *Trans Day of Revenge* (2016)

Coco Rosie – *We Are On Fire* (2012)

Bikini Kill – *Yeah Yeah Yeah* (2014, re-issue of recordings made in 1991-1992)

Madonna – *True Blue* (1986)

Barbie – *Trimmen met Barbie* (1982)

Vive La Fête! – *Schwarzkopf* (2014)

LBL Feat. Princess Superstar – *Goes Busters* (2006)

The Girls' Room also features work by Daantje Bons, Camille Auer and Nasty Women, go to page 145 for more info ❤

Introduction by Pernilla Ellens

Mermaid leather & drink-straw dresses

Pernilla Ellens

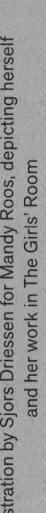

Illustration by Sjors Driessen for Mandy Roos, depicting herself and her work in The Girls' Room

Mandy Roos is working as a freelance fashion designer and interior stylist, while also specialising in textile practices. Inspired by science fiction, daily life and patterns of gendered expectations the designs of Roos are beautiful but strange. In her work, the tension between tactility and reluctance is ever present. Roos plays with the expectations of everyday objects and unexpected materials.

Mermaid leather & drink-straw dresses

The designs produced are both domestic and haute couture. At first glance, the works of Roos seem cheeky and incite you to touch, play with and feel the various fabrics and materials. Yet, upon closer inspection, the decorative objects and wearable interior applications tickle you to think about the relationships between object and subject, material and function. Mandy exhibited a number of her autonomous pieces in The Girls' Room. She created all of the textile designs, such the pink fur upholstery, the soft baby blue nipple-shaped bed sheet, and the squeaky, fake-leather mermaid-like cushions. She has payed special attention to the layering of different materials, colours and textures in order to create the perfect girly bedroom. Visitors could touch everything and were invited to chill on the bed or the seats, to read from the library, listen to the records or just to hang out during events at Onomatopee.

YOUNG GIRL, THEY CALL THEM THE DIAMOND DOGS

As well as making specific interior objects, Mandy filled the room with furniture from both second-hand stores and IKEA, just like a young girl might assemble her room. The main wall was covered with a pink holographic, mirroring material. Placed in front of it was a heart-shaped pink neon lamp, especially designed for The Girls' Room by Eindhoven based neon artist Munne. The mirror and lamp combo scattered light onto the artworks as well as the visitors, who saw themselves reflected into the exhibition. By night, the main light went off but the neon one stayed on, leaving a curious glow in the room. Because of its reflection onto the holographic mirror wall, it created a specific effect, a shade of green light juxtaposed to the blue and pink scheme. Next to the neon-lamp, the room was lit by bright blue and intense pink fluorescent lights, usually used in clubs and gas stations. The chosen colours for the lights corresponded to the two binary genders and their attributed symbols, whilst the fluorescent effect contributed to the young, bright, teenage feel. In its physicality, the bed is just a wooden structure with textile layering, platonically referring to the idea of the designed bed. In Mandy's realm, it became the perfect teenage hang-out with phallus shaped cuddly cushions and soft pink fur sheets. For The Girls' Room, the collection *Softie Wanted* (created by Mandy together with another Eindhoven based designer Victoria Ledig) was expanded with two new works, commissioned by Onomatopee. The blue and purple rectangular shaped rug with smaller cubicles on top, was placed in the middle of the room on a plinth, becoming the abstract centrepiece of the show. The magenta piece, with its nipple-like structure was placed in the corner on the bed, with its round, curved shape somewhat resembling kissing lips. Both rugs were made with foam and sprayed with a flock technique, thus becoming something that both touches and is touchable. The rugs' function in the room were as autonomous objects as well as interior decorations.

BARBARELLA AND BODY HAIR

Softie Wanted More, also created in cooperation with Victoria, as well as *Trichophilia*, part of Mandy's graduation work, were already existing works, newly exhibited in The Girls' Room. They gained a new function as part of the teenage girl narrative. The sculpture Softie Wanted More becomes a Bowie-esque uniform, a dress expressing a futuristic extravaganza par excellence. It is perfect for a night of dressing up in your room, feeling wonderful and excited.

The two little undies, part of the work *Trichophilia*, celebrates body hair in a playful way. For many young girls, body hair is a big issue. Media, men and women trapped in patriarchal beauty standards direct us to either shave it off or to hide it. However, body hair, and especially pubic hair, is part of our natural bodies and even who we are. So, why should we feel ashamed of it and conceal its existence? *Trichophilia* is a good example of autonomous work raising questions around the theme of the project, while at the same time fitting perfectly into the chosen aesthetic of the The Girls' Room.

Furthermore, the room featured a desk, a reading corner, and a listening station. A little drawer inside the desk featured gem stones, gay condoms, shiny stickers and

Mermaid leather & drink-straw dresses

business cards. There was also a diary with a fluffy baby blue pen, where everyone was invited to write their deepest thoughts surrounding the theme. These ranged from: *I just bought a drill and now I feel manly. Is this a problem?* to *I want to have anal sex but my boyfriend thinks it's gay*. Next to the books on the shelve, a sex toy was placed. Posters of the space queen Barbarella and feminist academic De Beauvoir adorned the walls, alongside the casual *Gender Liberation Now!* slogan. On a pin-board, some pictures of the SS logo and models were hung, with little snippets of texts showing biographies of the contributing artists and information about their work, all riso-printed on blue and pink paper.

From the magenta sausage-patterned rug lying in the corner of the bed, to the indigo and purple textured object in the middle of the room, to the pink-and-blue dress made of straws, the babypink fake-fur upholstery and the blue nipple-textured bedding, to the leatherlike seat cushions, Mandy's use of textile is various, surprising and a result of what craftmanship and commissioned work can look like in an autonomous form. Her tactile pieces fit perfectly into the concept of The Girls' Room, but remain their own aesthetic with original intrinsic qualities.

By adding pieces like *Trichophilia* to the room, even more reflection on the theme by means of showing the work takes place. By choosing specific wall-ornaments, lighting and the careful placement of the other artworks in the room, Mandy created not only a bedroom for the project, but she let the visitor peek into her own world as well. Within her work and her design for The Girls' Room, Mandy has given all the bad girls, good girls, and all other gender identities visiting Onomatopee a warm, soft and playful welcome.

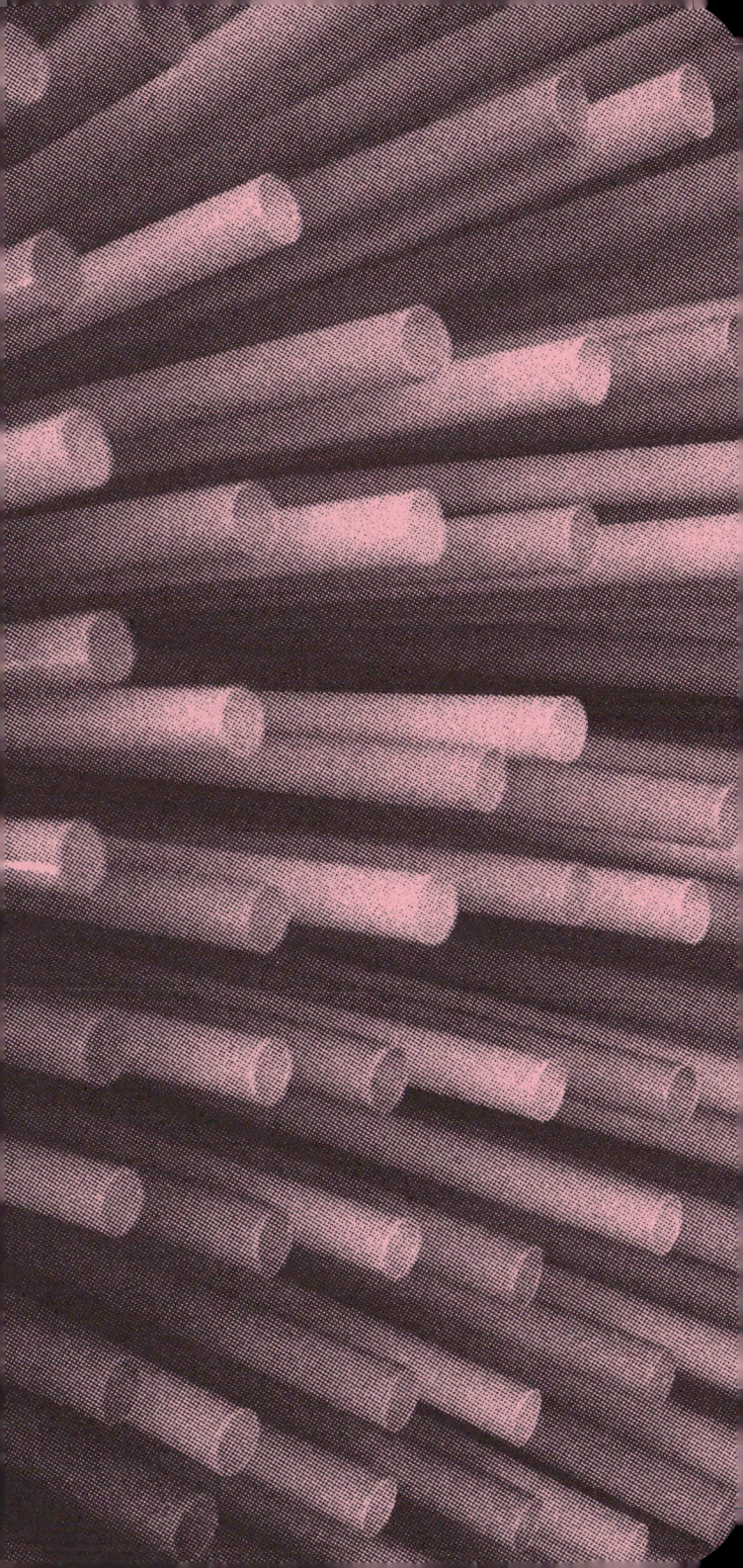

Gabriel A. Maher, Roberto Pérez Gayo & Carly Rose Bedford

"

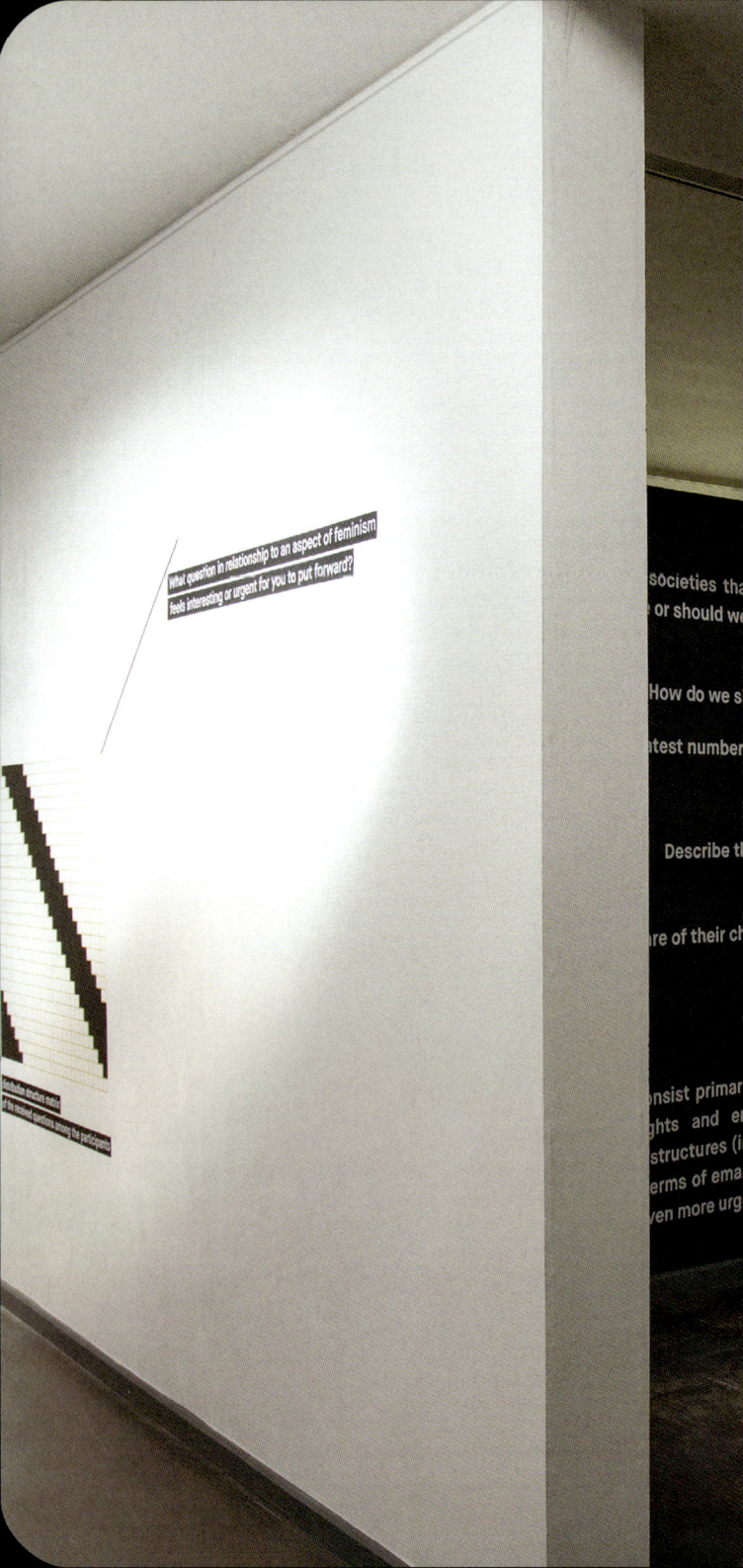

d the patriarchal, racist and
ore 'ground zero' situation by

preserve agency while acknowledging victimization?

h you and your lover last left each other.

at least as much of men than of women? The idea that
s outdated in our current society. But if we see
stitutions, or daily practice), aren't men, here and today,
gender stereotypes? For instance: if girls must dare to
allowed to have the ambition of becoming a housekeeper

How can feminism, as

Combining thoughts, questions and e
humans / world citizens without racis

What role does popular cult

As a trans woman, sometimes I fe

In r

Can we consider that, in the conte
spread an idea of collaboration be

Which vocabularie

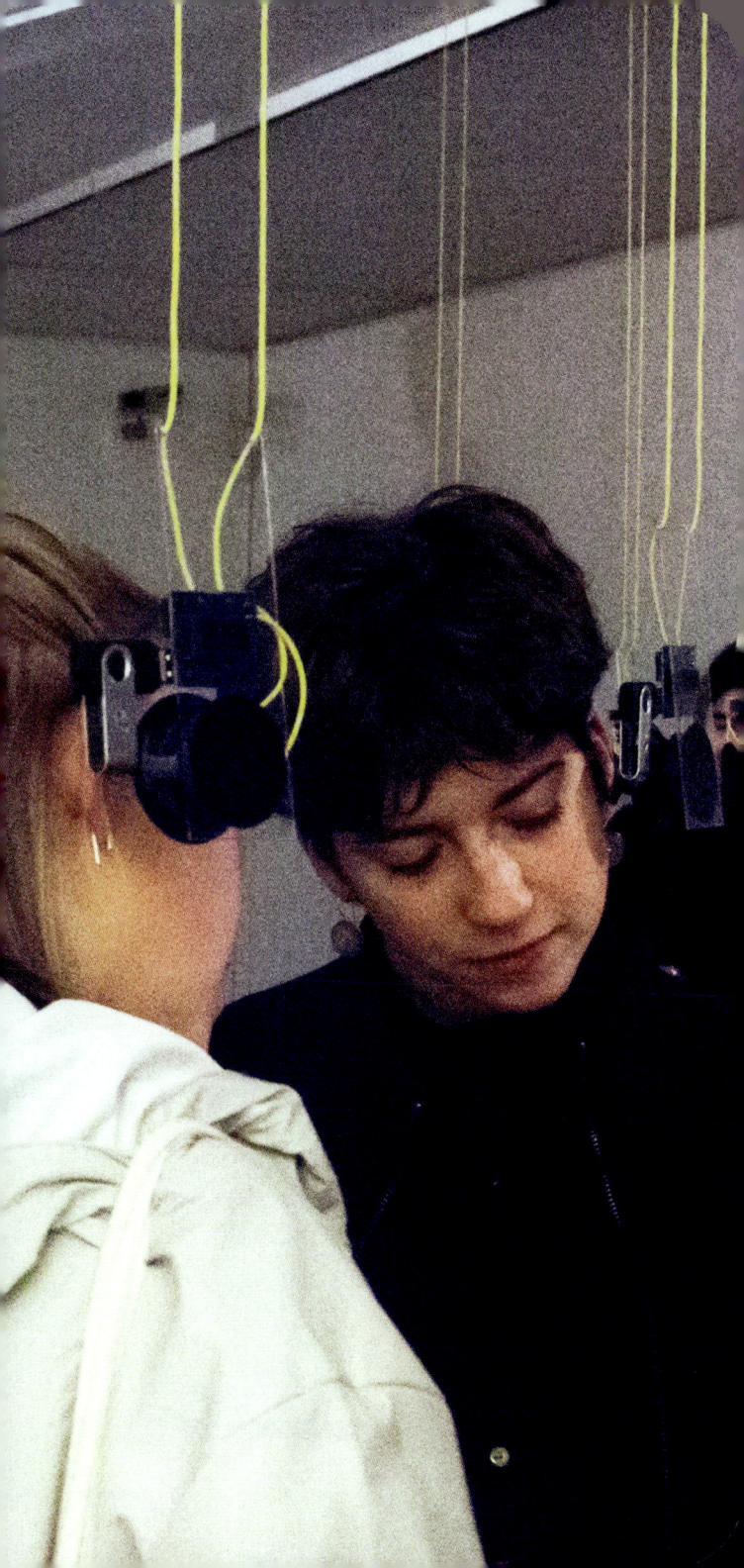

tling white supremacy in our global soc

Toni Morrison, one could ask the question,

w complicit is architecture within larger power structures tha
e built environment through spatial planning and professional

bei   out of the conversation?

that it's so easy to devalue my opinion on the

etymological level, seems exclusive and d

How can

My question is (addressed to non-hu
communities live by and share or diff

distance

Sense & Sensibility n°2 — *Introduction by* *Gabriel A. Maher, Roberto Pérez Gayo & Carly Rose Bedford* — October 17

"   "

_____

7 October 2017 – 12 November 2017

04.09.2017 – Unpublished Long Version of the Work Intentions.

As response to the invitation for a show in Onomatopee, we intend to produce a collaborative body of work that researches the relationship of feminism to the collective regimes of enunciation that produce it. From this angle, we approach feminism as a word, and as such as, a technology with the capacity for ordering.

–

Investigating the word as technology allows us to look at language not only as a representational and communicational tool, but as one of order. As a word, feminism functions as a term with the capacity to (re)produce an assemblage of bodies, knowledge and actions endowed with agency to question, contest and perforate systems of power through visibility and collectivity. We are interested precisely in the formation of these collectivities and how our individual positions and actions relate to these collective arrangements through the word feminism.

–

We choose to research the word as a technology because we understand that repetition and redundancy are features that play important role in the production of communities. This becomes particularly interesting when taking into consideration how in language the individual enunciations get lost in the collective social landscape and how in a back and forth movement individuals can become vehicles for these collective arrangements, now encapsulated within a word.

Unpublished Long Version of the Work Intentions

We are interested in exploring the effects that repetition in feminism has, it's capability to empower communities, to bring them together and to create spaces of resistance. In our work together we want to understand how we can orient ourselves within a language that precedes us, in the spaces that open in front of us. We want to understand how we are transformed and affected, both when the word feminism passes through us and we enter inside of it, and to listen to the echoes that resonate once the word fades.

—

We are interested in the word feminism because it invites us to listen.

—

Feminism as a word has the capacity to transform its own conditions and function as a disruptive agent within the linguistic regime. Feminism as a word has the capacity to shatter itself into pieces and break apart the monopoly of universal signification, to interrogate the power structures that exists within itself and the ones in which it exists. Feminism as a word has the potential to challenge its own material and its own historical tendencies. And the condition required for this to happen is listening.

—

In our research we want to emancipate listening from a passive subjected position of reception and instead we want to assert it as an active force in culture and in collective and individual politics. We want to speculate on how setting up the listening conditions before talking can generate new forms of community and collectivities and how collective listening can contribute to challenge systems of power and generate self reflection.

Introduction by Gabriel A. Maher, Roberto Pérez Gayo & Carly Rose Bedford

We want to question whose voice is listened to and whose agency is given to whom within feminism. In our work together we want to raise as many voices as possible without having to find resolution in a single and unique voice. Therefore, we aim to stay in an ever-changing, balancing space that requires from us a constant reorientation through listening to our surroundings. We want to listen to the word feminism trough intersectionality and queer theory. We want explore how its volume, its texture and colour changes, how it distorts when spoken at the same time, how it diversifies and how it changes in return the spaces it resonates within.

–

If we look from this perspective to the word FEMINISM, we can see within its translucent walls a universe contained, a constellation of bodies, expressions, qualities and territories. The word itself becomes a door to a sonic space in which a certain types of relations happen and are expressed in a particular form, enabling us to occupy a physical and mental space.

–

Once I cross into that space,
how do/can/must/may/ought 'I' move/relate/interact/feel?
And how would I describe it?

About Gabriel A. Maher, Roberto Pérez Gayo & Carly Rose Bedford

Gabriel A. Maher (1983, AUS)

Gabriel A. Maher is a designer currently living and working in the Netherlands, having received her Master Social Design diploma in 2014 from Design Academy Eindhoven. Until 2012, Maher practiced and taught interior architecture and design in Sydney and Melbourne, Australia. With a background in interior architecture, Maher's practice is essentially focused on relationships between body and structure, with an interest in objects and systems. An emerging methodology seeks to create situations where research and design come together in performance. Questioning design and media practices through queer and feminist frameworks is a core position and approach. Their* investigations confront a range of intersectional concerns, which frame concepts of gender, race, and class as well as highlight how the body, identity, and subjectivity are positioned, organized and managed through design and media systems.

*Pronouns: They/them/theirs

Roberto Pérez Gayo (1983, ES)

As a designer and social worker, Roberto Pérez Gayo explores the potentialities that run beneath our constructed cultures. Roberto explores subjectivity as the elaboration of a system that allows the controlling of its own operations; something that modifies itself by inventing new internal structures, and generates its own mode of addressing problems. Integral to this subjectivity is a task that is never completed and is always in the process of becoming more and other. It is a subjectivity that travels away from the center of power and political life and becomes the condition under which social and collective life arises.

Carly Rose Bedford (1983, AUS)

Carly Rose is a multidisciplinary artist who works across a diverse spectrum of mediums from performance, to sculptural installations, to text. Their work encapsulates an obsessive meditation on how materials stimulate an affective response within the body, and its collision with queer praxis by employing questions of aesthetics, taste, camp and confusion as a language that can subvert or disrupt hierarchy. Paralleling their studio practice, Carly Rose has an ongoing research project that focusses on how queer artists use nature as a site of potentiality and resistance to dominant normative structures.

Methodological considerations

Gabriel A. Maher
Roberto Pérez Gayo
Carly Rose Bedford

The project with which we have responded to the invitation by Onomatopee to contribute to their Sense and Sensibility project had from the very beginning a double intention. The first one, saw our work materialising into the creation of a sonic installation that researched on the multiplicity of positions from which feminism can be lived. The second, which was actually, where a majority of the labour ended up being invested, was to develop a methodology of work aligned to the feminist principles we practice and through which we could articulate the collaborations necessary to produce the above-mentioned installation. This double approach is a commonality all three of us share in our individual practices, one of being led by research and seeing this as a concrete material of our practice and our lives.

Departing from a speculation on the politics of listening and its capacity to generate new forms of community, we investigated which pre-existing power structures were embedded and inherent to the way we communicated and generated work, be that through language, decision making or the normalized dynamics that exist within institutionalized systems in general. A large part of feminism is based in dismantling hierarchical and oppressive structures that exist, not only in relationship to gender politics but also to how they are enacted within social life in general. This is why aspects such as language choice and institutional critique within our writing, correspondence and methodology occupied such a prominent space, with the hope that we could find ways to tackle these issues on a broader scale from a grass roots position.

Embodying these politics demanded a critical approach that lead us to explore new ways of integrating these principles.

Methodological considerations

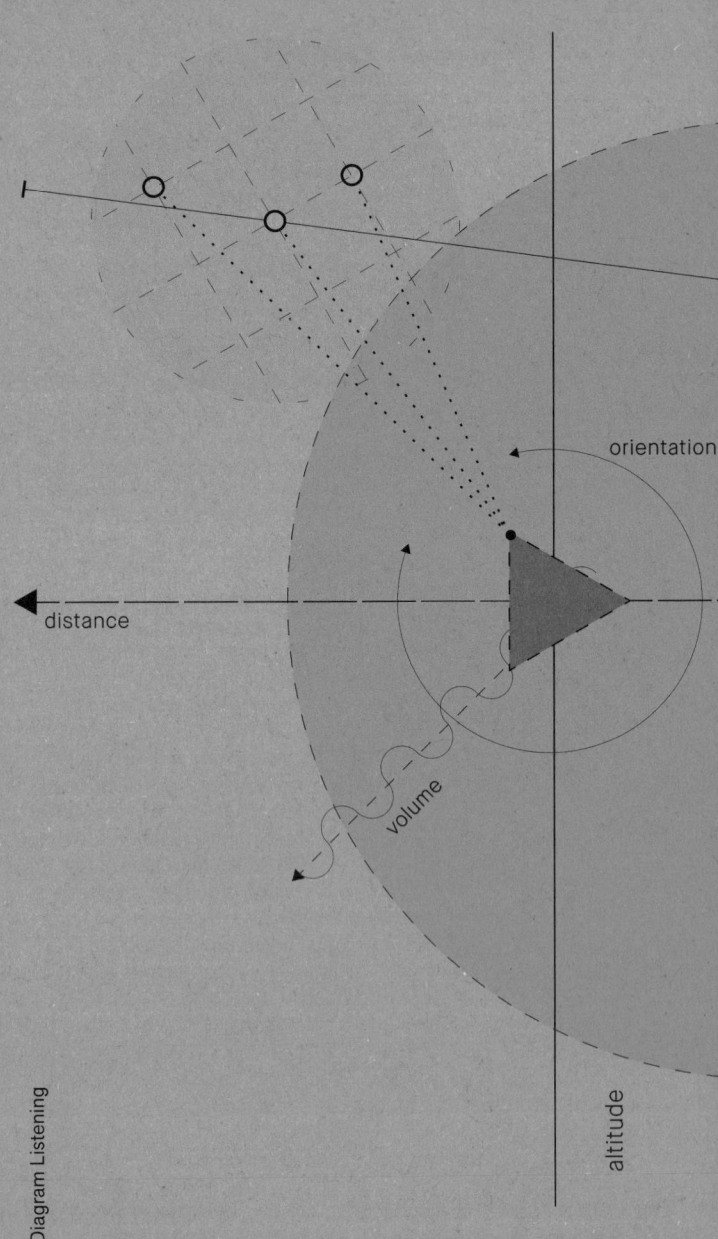

Diagram Listening

Sense & Sensibility nº2 — Gabriel A. Maher, Roberto Pérez Gayo & Carly Rose Bedford — October 17

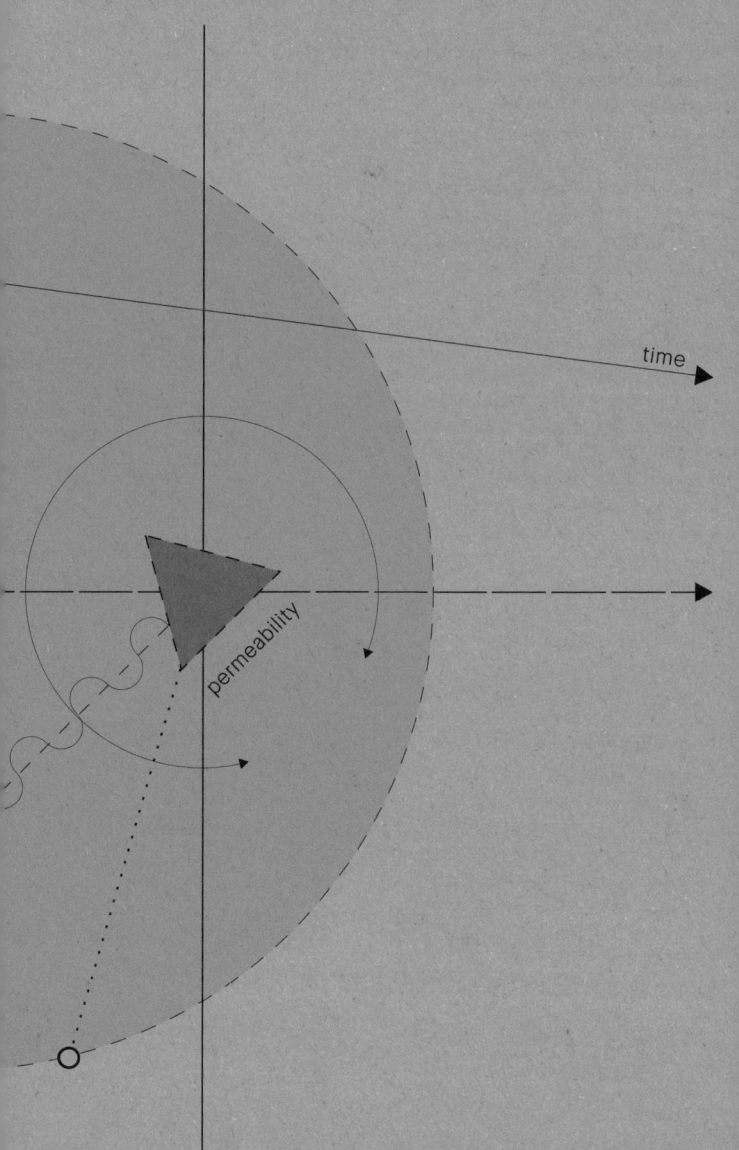

Methodological considerations

Furthermore, it invited us to practice transparency and vulnerability as strategies. These politics and strategies would allow us to remain faithful to how we perceived and approached working as a collective on the subject of feminism.

Each of the following extracts is part of an archive of collectively written texts throughout the project. Following the same transparency that we committed to during our collaboration, and taking into consideration how crucial the development of this methodology has been for the work itself, and for us as artists/designers/activists, we have decided to include in this publication some of the correspondence we maintained with the contributors to our installation.

Avoiding a more didactic approach to the transmission of our communication that would require a publication on itself, we thought it best to make a selection of emails/writing 'behind the scenes' accessible as this is where a majority of our labor was driven. It was in our writing and communication to others where we had to constantly question our intentions, equality and values, right down to the language that we chose, which was constantly influenced by a return to and evaluation of what it means to produce a work about feminism.

In the form of footnotes to the correspondence, we have decided to incorporate some clarifications to the terminology and language that we deployed in our communication. With this gesture we would like to emphasize how the process and nature of our work, and the topics upon which we touch, still offer space for further consideration. Testimony to this are the conversations sparked by these texts that we are sharing with the institution that houses us while this publication ultimates its last details.

We have the opportunity to continue working with Onomatopee in finding structures in which our own categories, frames and expectations can find a temporary suspension, a space in which to share, articulate and reorient our positions. Critique is a challenge to give and receive. It is for this reason that we are currently researching and discussing with them about creating spaces for listening, recognition, attention and negotiation we can create together and within institutional systems.

We would like to invite you to consider the following texts not only as a documentation, but as the starting point of a new phase in our work and our institutional collaborations.

Sense & Sensibility n°2 *Gabriel A. Maher,*
Roberto Pérez Gayo
& Carly Rose Bedford

Dear _____ ,

We can't emphasize enough how humbled we feel by your participation. Thank you so much for submitting your question and bringing your voice into this project.

We are moved by the numerous and enthusiastic response that our invitation has received. A total of twenty-six voices will resonate together. This is exciting! However, this volume makes us aware that inviting you to respond to each of the questions would demand from your side an enormous investment. It is for this reason that we would like to invite you to respond to only six of them.

We have distributed the totality of the questions into twenty-six different sets, each unique for every participant. By doing this we ensure that every question receives the same amount of answers. Next to this, with this gesture we avoid structuring the voices into groups or topic areas, embracing in this way all the complexity and diversity of this work. At this point, the questions that you receive do not include the name of the participants who generated them. By doing this we would like to propose that you consider each of the questions on their own terms and leave out of the answering process any external system of value that might endow some of them with more or less weight than others.

These are the six questions that we would like to share with you:

[...]

In the next page you will find our availability in the coming weeks so that we can arrange with you a moment in which to record the answers. We would appreciate very much if you could offer us more than one possibility. This would facilitate greatly our capacity to accommodate all the participants. If you have any questions or comments, please do not hesitate in contacting us.

Thank you very much in advance.
Looking forward to the comings steps,

Gabriel A. Maher, Roberto Pérez Gayo
& Carly Rose Bedford

Methodological considerations

Where in your body does your rage reside? What is its weight, volume a[nd...]

Can we consider that, in the context of an intersectional fight f[or...] and does not spread an idea of collaboration between individu[als...]

How do we simultaneously preserve agency wh[ile...]

How can we queer the norm without posing a new norm?

What is our duty as feminists towards a future,
what does a feminist future look like?

Can you tell me of a moment when you got aware of one or sever[al...]

Which vocabularies do we choose when we articulate our works to others?

Feminism is transient and contextual, however, can we envision a [...] in society's collective values, or will it perpetually re-emerge and [...]

Combining thoughts, questions and expressions of feminists Anja Meulenb[elt...] one could ask the question, "What are we / people / humans / world citizer[s...]

As a trans woman, sometimes I feel less allowed to have a voice [...] my opinion on the grounds of my biological gender. How does yo[u...]

Shouldn't the next generation of feminist consist primarily of men? But if we see feminism as dismantling oppressive gender structure[s...] emancipation from gender stereotypes? For instance: if girls must [...] when they are grown?

I work in a shelter for homeless people. The vast majority of our guests in this men's world? Should I focus on the minority of female visitors? Those 3 positions conflict- or should they not?

xture? Are you a woman? How do you know?

uality, the word Feminism, on an etymological level, seems exclusive gardless of gender?

How complicit is architecture within larger power structures that facilitate people in the built environment through spatial planning and professional

knowledging victimization?

y question is (addressed to non-human and human animals including plants hics or values that your communities live by and share or differ on?

What single change in the world

your privileges?

How can feminism, as a tool or methodology, work towards dismantling

ealistic future where feminism is a non-issue as it becomes ingrained incarnate as another issue without solutions?

Should we use violence to force change? OR What methods racist and heterosexual that inhabit our minds and bodies? more 'ground zero' situation by 'overthrowing' institutions?

d Toni Morrison,
thout racism, sexism and classism?"

What are the ways gender non-conforming identities

Why there is always a nursing room with the woman image / logo on it?

ninine subjects, or, I feel that it's so easy to devalue
ninism respond to this position?

In a society where people affected by systemic oppressions justify, or defend their experience and knowledge when they

at least as much of men than of women? The idea that feminism is primarily discourse, institutions, or daily practice), aren't men, here and today, the re to dream to become head of police, shouldn't, even more urgently, boys

are men. As a women, should I stand strong
And should I be gender-neutral in the team?

Are non-white women still being left out of the conversation?

exclusion and violence against queer and gender nonconforming
practice?

and other elemental beings): Do you have social

would, in your opinion, improve life for the greatest number of women?

white supremacy in our global social and political climate?
What role does popular culture play in contemporary feminism?

can we think of to establish societies that leave behind the patriarchal,
Must we be willing to work for gradual change or should we strive for a

disrupt the current theories and politics of feminism?

Shouldn't men take care of their children too?

are constantly expected to explain, demonstrate, prove, discuss,
speak up, I wonder, is pedagogy inherent to feminism?

about women's rights and emancipation is outdated in our current society.
ones that have the most work to do, in terms of
be allowed to have the ambition of becoming a housekeeper and good fath

Sense & Sensibility n°2 *Gabriel A. Maher, Roberto Pérez Gayo & Carly Rose Bedford*

During the process of receiving questions, several important points were also raised, which related to our frameworks and institutional critique. We feel that these points are important to answer to you collectively because they incited a further reflection toward our own position and a clarification of certain aspects of the project.

A central part of this process has been to actively embed a working methodology that reflects non-hierarchical approaches to collectivity and remaining accountable during the entire process of generating this work.

The first of these reflections involves transparency of budget. This project has received a relatively minimal budget. We initiated this project knowing that its value lay not in a monetary gain but in the opportunity to put forward a gesture that was strong in its position, generous in what it could pedagogically and artistically offer and reflective of accountability towards the institution that houses it.

In total, we received a budget of 750 euros. This is inclusive of all material, production, transportation and miscellaneous costs. We are aware that we have asked for your labours without a monetary contribution. Our intention is to apply for additional funding in the hope to retroactively pay you for the time and energy invested in the project. Your contribution is important to us and we understand that compensation for a project that is housed inside an institution is an important political gesture as a ballast to so many institutions demanding free labour for activist/political or artistic work in exchange for visibility.[1]

Our second point to follow up is how we are considering the relationship of the project to the institution itself.

Up until this point, your names have not been given to the gallery since we did not have a definitive list of contributions until last Tuesday. After several discussions, we have considered proposing to not disclose your names to the institution for this particular show in relation to your contribution to this project. We have problematised how institutions in general can commodify and claim the content of activist/political work, and people involved, as a way of accruing political and discursive capital without accountability or engagement with what we believe to be some fundamentals of feminist politics.

Methodological considerations

In this way, your voices will be transmitted into the space, without attaching them to your name and identity. This gesture intends to evade any institutional claim to your contribution or work/person/identity as a way of evidencing the institution's participation in feminist or queer politics now or in the future while also maintaining the capacity of the work to reach the public, and transmit the message. From the perspective of the visitor, this will permit an experience of the work without any pre-given value to any of the content.[2]

Having said this, if the work is presented in the future, within a different context or under different conditions, we would ask for your permission to run the project with your names acknowledged.

Please let us know if you have any further considerations or comments on the proposal not to disclose your names. We'd be very happy for your feedback on this point. Finally, we were also asked several questions about diversity within the project. We were attentive to include as many people from as many positions as possible within this project, be that race, sexual orientation, class, gender + and how these intersect with each other to form a constellation of diversity.

Diversity itself is a word that is constantly problematised, especially in relationship to institutional representation. We considered the importance of this and our role as mediators of your voices. The possibility of 'evidencing' diversity is something we actively wanted to avoid. In our labours, we were aware of our position in collecting voices around a subject as loaded as feminism due to its current/historical relationship with inclusivity, diversity and representation. So again, while potentially not including your name in this iteration of the event publicly, we would not include any aspect of your identity for the same reasons. After the recent developments in the context in which we will work, we are working on strategies on how to emphasize institutional accountability.

If there are any comments, please do not hesitate to send them. We would be happy to collect them all and answer collectively to them.

1.

This paragraph regards our accountability for not financially compensating for the time/contributions from our participants. We understood from the beginning that the budget of 750 given by Onomatopee as an independent institution was for a solo show. However, we actively decided to open up this invitation to more contributors, since our intention was always to approach feminism from as many positions as possible, as we understand feminism as complex and multiple. Being aware, as we were, of the above conditions, this passage explains our intended use of the 750 euros we were given and explores what options were, and still are, being considered for compensating our extended network of contributions retroactively.

Next to this, having worked on many projects that uphold this politics of transparency, we decided to disclose this information, as it is common practice to either out rightly share budget information or be asked to do so.

We consider free labour a crisis within creative culture and even though we were asking for it ourselves, we wanted to make sure there was a sufficient ballast to that in return. Hence, being transparent about budget sharing, where we were positioned and what we were gaining on a concrete and material level.

2.

In this paragraph, we reflect further on a larger context. This felt of extreme urgency taking into consideration our community experiences of how the institutional systems can generally capitalise on diversity and minoritarian/activist voices, in this particular case, institutions that program around feminist, queer, intersectional topics/artists and as such do not necessarily work from any binding feminist framework.

As we mentioned in previous instances, this project had two outcomes running parallel. One was to create a materialised outcome. The second was to work rigorously with feminist politics and develop a methodology that, not only aligned with this project but that we could continue to work within for future projects as well.

As heavy or as blunt as critique might seem at first, this practice is always valuable and we felt it important to lay it as a foundation of our working methodology. Institutional critique is part of a broader canon of criticality that analyses, dissects and problematises structural or hierarchical executions of power on many levels. Implementing this within our work is personal as well as political. We have all experienced these hierarchies on various levels and as such, chose to embody critical analysis and active processes of disruption in the way we live as well as through our practices. Alternatively, this has opened a space of questioning, reflection and dialogue together with Onomatopee, which highlights the potential for a productive and mutually constitutive relationship between activism and institutional critique/institutional systems.

Methodological considerations

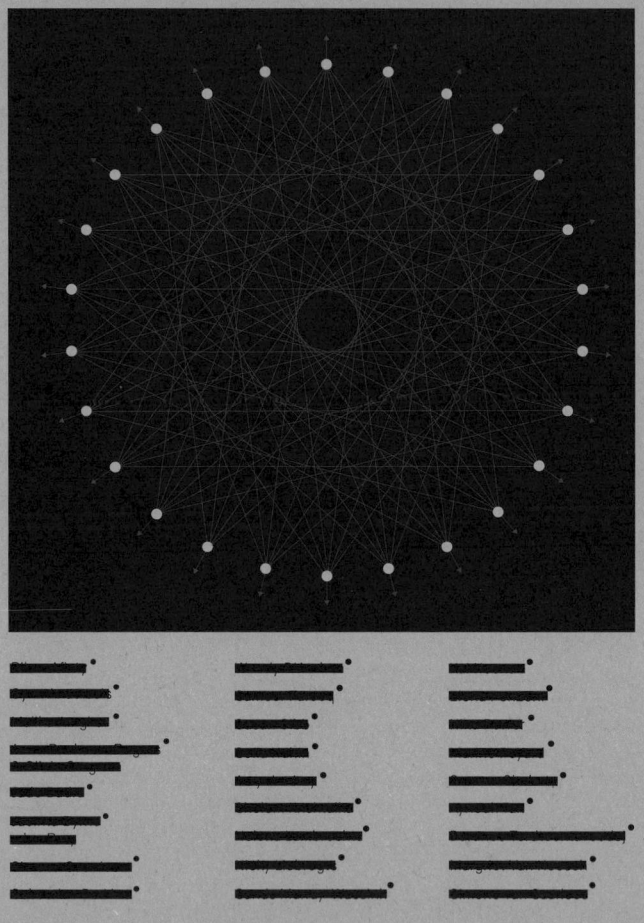

We would like to thank the 26 participants who contributed their voices to this work / Amsterdam - Rotterdam - Eindhoven - Berlin - London - Gothenburg - Stockholm - Jakarta - Toronto - Kingston - Melbourne - Sydney - Newcastle / Photography: Kyle Tryhorn and Daantje Bons. Tech-development + production: Isabel Mager

Nina Power wrote a contextual reflection of the work by Maher, Gayo and Bedford called The Politics of Pitch. Go to page 167 to read it ❤

Olle Lundin Bureau Just

Bureau Just
Agency for Feminist Practices

Pernilla Ellers
Executive Producer

Bureau Just
Agency for Feminist Practices

Josh Plough
Hospitality Assistant

Bureau Just
Agency for Feminist Practices

Freek Lomme
Head of Security

This badge gives exclusive permission to enter the Body Bureau ©
SENSE & SENSIBILITY

"My utopia is social and emotional justice"

"What I mean is not the prevention of rights"

"But real rights"

"We need to stop blaming the victims and make sure that everyone is a part of the movement."

"All employers need a feminist agenda."

"It's a mindset, content awareness will bring change, in some way education"

"I don't think I understood that it was sexism"

"Having the same possibilities and the same opportunities."

"Objectification doesn't always have to be bad, if Kim Kardashian is owning her fame and is the one benefiting from it, isn't that pro-active?"

"I don't know you, you can dance with me but you can't touch me"

"With feminism you are opening up the pathway, not only for others but for yourself as well"

" I see discrimination when someone is put out because of gender, race or sexual orientation but I still think discrimination is so incorporated that it has become invisible, it has become normal almost as a role-game in life, or as in 'nature'"

" The main point is to reach a kind of awareness around men, and what issues to men have? We have the period, what is the your 'thing' what makes you angry once or twice a month? What hormones are going around inflicting your emotions?

Just tell   ıt's a become

" It's a mindset, constant awareness will bring change, but in some kind of jobs it will take a long

" I don't think I understood that it was sexism"

"Objectification doesn't always have to be bad, if

to become second nature"

"For the structural change to happen, the old system has to retire before a more diverse and equal system can come in place, it's an unfortunate delay."

Introduction by Pernilla Ellens

Bureau Just: Agency for Feminist Practices

9 November 2017 – 9 December 2017

According to Olle Lundin, the rationality of us is but an illusion. We are all culturally prompted by society to mirror and reflect behaviour, and to act on the already well-trodden paths of our gender, class, or whatever else might constitute an identity. Through his work, Lundin wants to engage in conversations around equality, freedom, and respect in order to actively set an agenda in the city of Eindhoven.

For 2 days a week, Lundin was present in *Bureau Just* to conduct further research into social theory related to queering practices, feminism, equality, economy and class. This was combined with a field practice that collects auditive interviews to be archived into podcast-like segments. All the facilities needed were present at *Bureau Just*, temporarily transforming the exhibition into a research base. When not in use by Lundin, the visitor could see academic references, scribbles, and unanswered questions present in the bureau. The business element was used as a theme as the project sought to highjack elements of documentation and corporate-style strategy. The visual set-up of it drew on the formal aspects of a standardised office, therefore playing with the notions of normalcy, hierarchic structures and heteronormative work spaces. Through

About Olle Lundin

conducting interviews within Eindhoven, this project also engaged in the variety of social networks that constitute the city. All auditive interviews that were conducted in this research period have been documented at the website www.bureaujust.org. After *Bureau Just* had its first chapter at Onomatopee, Lundin seeks to further the research and project in the coming years.

Olle Lundin (1988, SE)

Through his work as a social designer, Olle Lundin investigates various social and political themes around gender, identity and the body. His projects materialize social theory and contemplate the norms of design and the social context in which it occurs. Lundin uses his own body as a means of communication, which he then uses to express critiques in outcomes as varied as body movement, experience design, fashion, performance and radio. Over the past year, Lundin has investigated how a museum collection can be viewed through a queer perspective and thereby questioning heteronormativity in art and society. Since his graduation in 2016 from the Design Academy Eindhoven, direction Man and Communication, Olle Lundin actively performs as a speaker and organizer of debates, reading groups and public events centered around gender issues.

Want to listen to Olle's interviews?
Go to www.bureaujust.org! ❤

Charlotte van Buylaere

Dear Olle

Charlotte van Buylaere

Moscow, 9 November 2017

Dear Olle,
How are you? Hopefully, you're not too stressed about the start of your research period at Onomatopee. I wish I could be there, but I'm currently on holiday in Moscow. I hope to visit your installation for Sense and Sensibility when I'm back in Western Europe. Say 'hi' from me to Pernilla and I wish to congratulate her on her curatorial work!

I've been thinking a lot about your work during my holiday, and based upon what you told me over the phone, I'd like to share some of my thoughts with you. I'm especially interested in the format of the interview you will use as the core of this project and I'm very fascinated by the way you strategically deploy body language – and often your own body – to instigate a critical discourse, in which social theories are materialised. Your communication design has little to do with the design of the

Dear Olle

external appearance of communication devices; instead it addresses speculative enquiries on symbolic interactions, social constructionism and different forms of talk or behaviour. The way you will collect thoughts and opinions on an actual feminist debate on inclusion and postcolonial legacies by instigating face-to-face interviews in the streets and at Onomatopee, is very intriguing. Centred upon the interview, this type of conversation becomes very ambiguous within your project, as it functions as both a designed communication format, a research methodology, a research object, a performance, an artwork, a tool or maybe even just the start of a further in-depth discussion. The interview becomes the source of political information; useful and desirable data which may provide interesting insights in local thought and geographic emancipation. Do you know the writings of Karen Barad? I think her conception of entangled agency and intra-action could be highly relevant for you to think about, or associate with your work.

In your previous work, Body Behaviour (2016), you analysed the various poses of models in fashion magazines. Reenacting the particular poses with your own body in a (quasi) reference-free space, you make the viewer aware of the culturally determined gender performativity and attempt to put this matter outside of the heteronormative matrix - if I may put it in Judith Butler's terminology :-). It

Charlotte van Buylaere

means that the beholder is challenged in perceiving the body in a non-biased manner without judging gender stereotypes. While your body operates as a generator of new meanings and affects your audience directly by means of your corporeality. You actually become one with the criticism of sexual difference theories and social normativity, and embody the social variability of sexes. Body Behaviour presents ideas on gender stereotypes in commercial communication, but it remains a one-way reception of an individual research. The project serves as an awareness campaign of the presence of biased messages in (commercial) communication, but doesn't really include interactivity with its audience. In this sense, I think Olle, that you instigate an interesting shift with your work Qwearing the Collection that you have been conducted together with Alice Venir at the Van Abbemuseum in Eindhoven. Herein you move the debate about gender, stereotypes and equality from the individual performance to a collective agency. The project aimed at breaking down heteronormative gender patterns depicted in paintings, sculptures and other artworks through a wearable gender neutral guide that incites the visitors to experience the collection from a peculiar feel and perspective. Also in this project, you focus on the body, where you allowed it to explore the collection within an interactive manner. There is a direct and physical communication between the collection and the beholder, however the audience is expected to take action in order to sense the effect.

And yet, I think that there is more to it than a sole interaction with the collection. Putting this design and the necessary action into a broader perspective, the writings of feminist scientist Karen Barad may offer compelling views to this matter. Drawing further on Judith Butler's conception of gender performativity, Barad sees bodies as always changing entangled agencies, adding matter to a certain phenomenon within the dynamic movement of intra-action. This is opposed to interaction as a form in which two pre-existing subjects interact with each other, but remain further as an independent subject with each of them their own agency, intra-action acts on the collective responsibility of humans and non-humans for the creation and existence of a phenomenon e.g. the concept of equality. Intra-action and entangled agency makes everything and everyone complicit in ethical and legal debates, but equally states that phenomena are not fixed but constant in change. Regarding the case of interviewing people on the street for Sense and Sensibility, this implies that interviews do not solely function as research materials, but operate as the true discourse on equality as such.

Interviewer and interviewees act on the mutual constitution of entangled agencies within the interview itself, and therefore they do not dis-

Charlotte van Buylaere

cuss the subject, but they become the subject. Even all the human and non-human things (gestures, smells, sounds, objects, feelings, voices, technology, waves, etc.) contribute to the very moment of the interview and simultaneously constitute the discourse. So I think we need to understand your role as the 'designer' as a kind of position in which one is aware of all these complicit beings. The fact that certain social roles and identities are performed and confirmed throughout the interview is a shared responsibility of the context and the persons involved. In other words, your share in this debate is not to ask citizens about equality, but you, together with everything around you, become the discourse about equality when you conduct the interview.

Assuming that we need to understand your work in this way, the discourse goes beyond a street talk about equal pay, the hijab debate or body hair removal (as possible subjects to start the debate with). Entangled agencies that are emphasised from within the interview create a new look at each move, each word, and all other non-human factors present in the context of the interview. Although as a designer, you cannot determine what the person will say to you, but you can influence the situation being fully aware of the whole context in which that interview takes place, including your own body. All of these human and non-human bodies create an 'apparatus of bodily production.'

Dear Olle

(Barad 2007: 206-218) After the bodily production that happens during the interview, you will then stage these recordings in the exhibition space. Karen Barad would coin these recorded sounds and words 'agential cuts,' because they make a cut between matter and meaning, sundering them or bringing them together. "Agential cuts are productive because they produce boundary-drawings that enable the analysis of new analytical entities of materiality and meaning." (Barad 2003, Posthumanist Performativity: 815) And therefore add content to the phenomenon.

So in fact, I'm very curious to hear from you how this debate on equality has evolved not only within the face-to-face interview, but rather as a general mode of awareness within Eindhoven and even beyond. Let's keep in touch about it!

Best wishes from Moscow!

Charlotte

REFERENCES

Barad K., Posthumanist Performativity: Towards an Understanding of How Matter Comes to Matter, in: Signs. Journal of Women in Culture and Society. Spring 2003, pp. 801-831

Barad K., Meeting the Universe Halfway: Quantum Physics and the Entanglement of Matter and Meaning, Duke University Press, 2007

Charlotte van Buylaere

Hey Olle, I think this quote by Michel Foucault that is written in his book Discipline and Punish *in 1975, makes total sense with respect to your work!*

"...the body is also directly involved in a political field; power relations have an immediate hold upon it; they invest it, mark it, train it, torture it, force it to carry out tasks, to perform ceremonies, to emit signs. [...] the body becomes a useful force only if it is both a productive body and a subjected body. This subjection is not only obtained by the instruments of violence or ideology; it can also be direct, physical, pitting force against force, bearing on material elements, and yet without involving violence; it may be calculated, organized, technically thought out; it may be subtle, make use neither of weapons nor of terror and yet remain of a physical order."

Bureau Just
Selected questions and answers

> How do you as a public figure deploy methods for gender equality?

"I try to organize events and groups outside of the heteronormative structure"

"Having the same possibilities and the same opportunities as everybody else"

Is there a policy against sexism at your work?

What is gender equality for you?

"I'm really campaigning, I'm a mother, and I have a daughter, so I'm worried about her future, I'm really trying to make men aware of what women are experiencing and that by accepting jokes and language around them it's becoming worse"

Bureau Just
Justify My Love

Olle Lundin
Charlotte van Buylaere
Pernilla Ellens

On a chilly Saturday on the 16th of December, Olle presented his research outcomes of Bureau Just to an audience at Onomatopee. Before the presentation started, the three of us sat down together to talk about the process of the research, the aims and goals of Bureau Just, and sexy chairs.

THE PROJECT

Charlotte: So, Olle, how did the project go?
Olle: It took some unexpected turns, which was nice. I focused more on the interviews than on getting further into academic writing. The interviews led straight from conversations into methods and actions, and that was nice to hear and to see, as it gave a lot more clarity to the project itself.
C: What do you mean by actions?
O: What people find necessary to do to stop sexual harassment, or to call out languagement, or to not laugh at jokes, because there is a darker undertone to those jokes and you might not realise at first. So a lot of that came pretty quickly as strategies let's say.

Bureau Just

Justify My Love

CONVERSATIONS

C: You prepared a couple of questions that you were asking to people in front of you. How did you manage to go immediately to a very interesting conversation, that didn't stay on the surface?

O: The different people that I interviewed were either from my personal surroundings, from my professional network or people on the streets. And those were really different kinds of interviews. Of course, on the street it's not super ethical to ask too direct questions. Which is different in a personal situation. So I think that also kind of led to which kind of questions could be asked. When it was a person in a power position, I wanted to know about policies and implementing their work to realise gender equality in the workplace, like "what do you do as a person?"

CITIZENS OF EINDHOVEN

C: Did you get some view on how feminist the people of Eindhoven are?

O: The citizens of Eindhoven were relatively a small group. But there were two things that I noticed in those interviews. Firstly, what happened a lot of times is that people got defensive and were like: "No my workplace is great, there are no problems". I think within the Dutch upbringing you have a kind of awareness about it, which is fine, but maybe we should implement policies. The other reaction that came out is that people were a bit surprised by the questions, but they were also happy to talk about it, they felt that it was important to do this, which was a nice revelation.

POLICIES AGAINST SEXISM

C: By policies, do you mean written policy rules against sexism at work?

O: Yeah. One example that came forward in the interviews is that we need to focus more on education and basically implementing this earlier. In another interview it came up that the Municipality of Eindhoven are implementing diversity policies in their ways of working and hiring. But of course it takes a bit of time before these kind of policies, or decision-making-structures, come in place. But then it's good to prepare towards them.

C: Yeah, but I still think there is a difference between having a diverse group of employees and a policy on sexist behaviour. You can have a very diverse group but still there can be a lot of sexism in that group.

O: Of course, but it's important to actively look for methods and strategies. I should actually go to the design academy and be like YO! You can also have some kind of cultural person-to-person thing, that's also important. But when you aim for key persons to interview who have the power to put things in motion, you can start a structural change.

DESIGNER

Pernilla: Olle, how did you feel doing this field research and empirical research as a designer?

O: It's interesting because with this project my design has been much more to engage, design has been actions to do things. As a designer, I see myself as an object with an agenda asking all these questions, and actively find people who have to use me. I have really appreciated that way of approaching the work. This project is going to travel to a lot of other things that I do, hopefully more explicitly as I've had a bunch of conversations so I know a bit more what I can do.

ON THE SPOT

C: Within the conversation, there are two layers. You have the spoken conversation, the words that are there, but you also have the behaviour within the conversation. It would be interesting to see how words respond within the people, in the gestures people were doing during the interview.

O: Yes very much, but unfortunately I didn't document that.

P: How people use their bodies when they are on spot and have to answer these questions is an important aspect

Justify My Love

of the strategy. That's what I found striking when you interviewed me Olle, I felt I had to be really sharp in my argument because I was on the spot. It's a bit like a Socratic dialogue. Just by asking questions, regardless the content of the questions, you already start to think. And make people more aware. I think this is the core of the project. Besides that, asking questions and getting answers is very performative.

BRIDGES INSTEAD OF LECTURES

P: I was also wondering if you experienced any difficulties with the people on the street to ask them if you could interview them?

O: I felt a bit of competition with people in the streets trying to sell you something, which was frustrating. But when I have the mic, and the questions and answers come and it gets recorded, it becomes real. The moment after the interview was often a really interesting moment to have a further discussion about things or I where could come with suggestions with what I think. And often I found those conversations more important and more fruitful for the meeting itself, than the interview. In a way the interview is a means to engage. And from there it develops and becomes more concrete even.

C: Did you notice a variety in the answers?

O: Yes very much, because all the people I was interviewing had a different understanding about feminism and the conversations were really different. Some of them were more intellectual and touching upon academia, some were more frustrated and some people just don't have a feminist agenda. They are maybe discriminated against in other ways, or were blind to privileges, so they don't care essentially. But they still need stepping stones to build on and they still need a bridge rather than a lecture. There, I was trying to ask the questions, listen and ask more questions, rather than explaining. Which was sometimes difficult, of course.

O. Lundin, C. Van Buylaere & P. Ellens

INTERVIEWING AS FEMINIST PRACTICE

P: Do you see this method of interviewing as a feminist practice?

O: Definitely, because the work that the Bureau is doing is to push for a feminist agenda, and to ask people questions about it. The questions and answers highlight the existence of discrimination, or the necessity for identity to be as fluent as possible, and not be stuck in stereotypes. I think those issues are central to the project.

P: But that's also the premise of the SS project, not to give feminism a new kind of stigma, but to make it as open as possible and give many people a platform to think about feminism, and how they would express it. Do you feel your feminism has changed by having the Bureau Just and doing all the interviews?

O: I feel that my feminism has become sharper, just by asking other people and putting them on the spot, I also have to be sharp. Engaging in conversations gave me a lot of clarity in what I can do and what I want to do, by being able to do this I realise I'm in a framework and I can put some of my attention to these strategies and try to work more with them.

EXPECTATIONS AND EXPERIENCE

P: Charlotte, what did you think about the project when you wrote your letter to Olle?

C: At the moment I was writing I didn't know about the questions, the setting, the frequency of Olle going into the streets. But I think the questions are touching upon really good things. Bureau Just feels a lot like a starting point that can be turned into a larger research project or a larger work. I think that's necessary to do. The interviews are asking for that.

P: In the beginning, Bureau Just was actually a conceptual thing. We talked about having this boring office, semi-criticising heteronormative office culture. But then because of Olle's dedication to the project, Bureau Just

Bureau Just
Justify My Love

became a real thing, instead of just an art installation, that's being activated by Olle asking questions.

C: It's good that you point out the heteronormative office, because we're talking about equality in this very hierarchical installation. Did you ever switch places with the interviewees?

O: No, but I felt very uncomfortable sitting behind the desk, haha. But indeed, the person who has the power and is asking the questions, is sitting behind the desk, in this leather and metal chair, putting gender equality on the agenda everyday, on every working hour of the bureau.

P & C: Its kind of sexy! (laughing)

O: Haha yes. But now, back to work!

Zarina Frye
People are not nowhere near so fluid

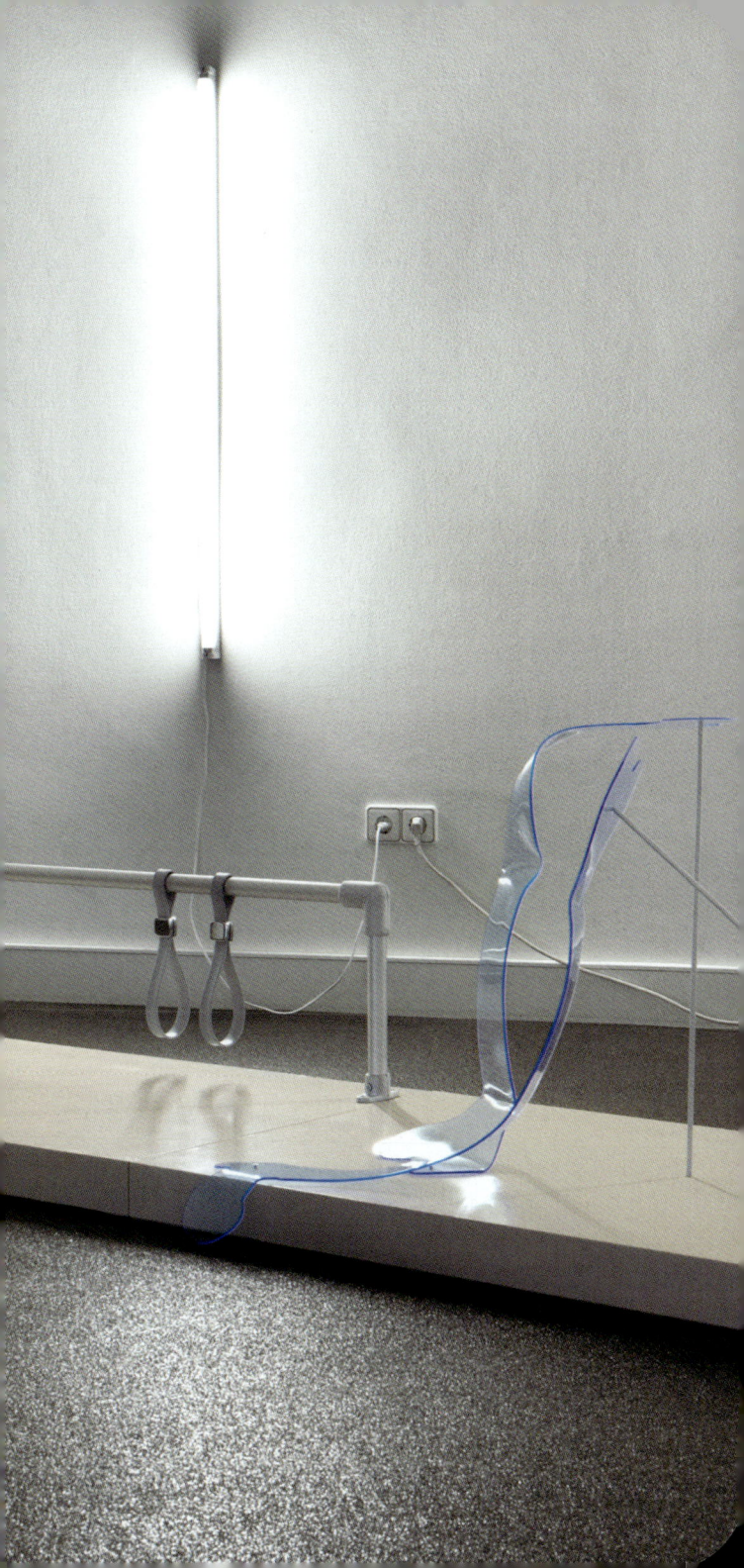

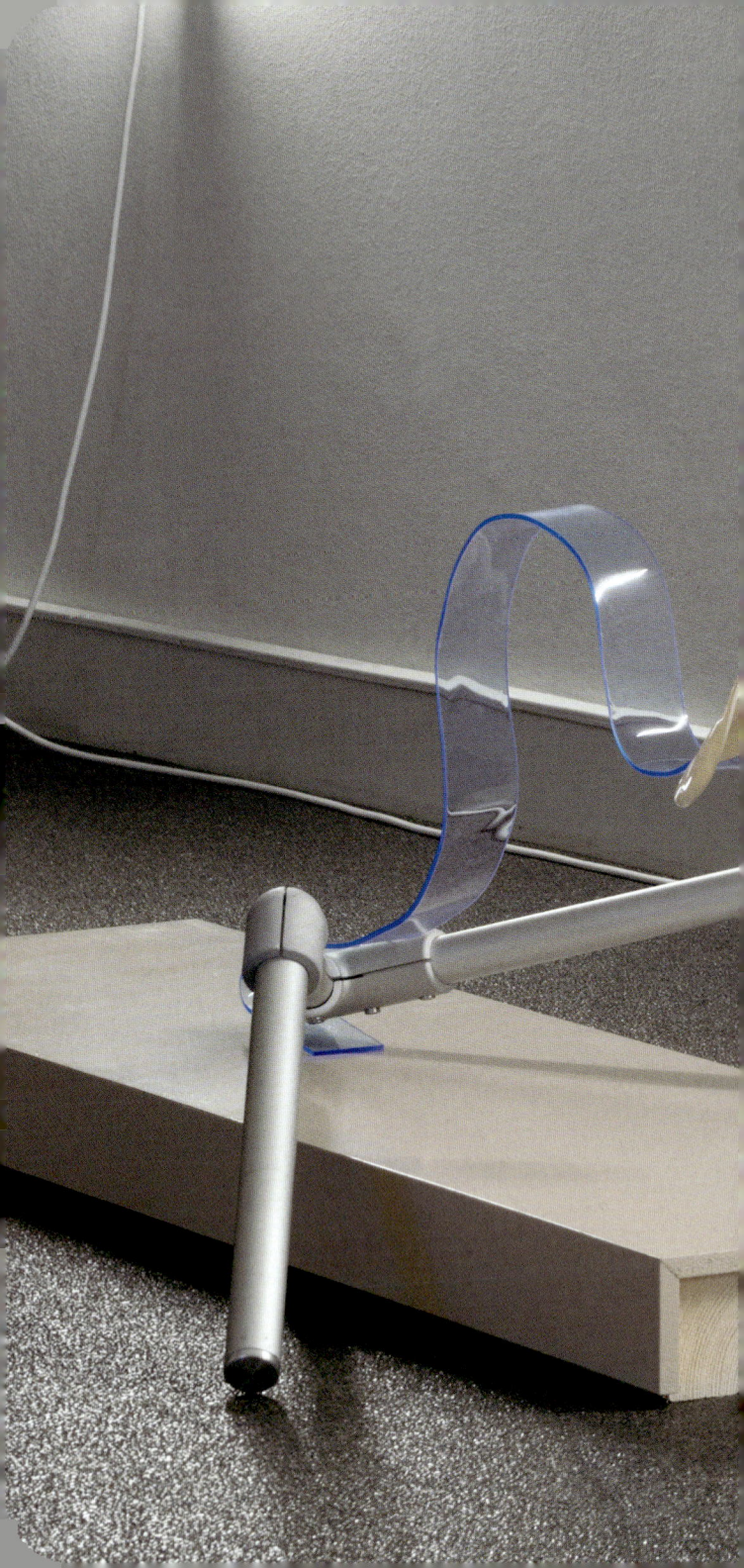

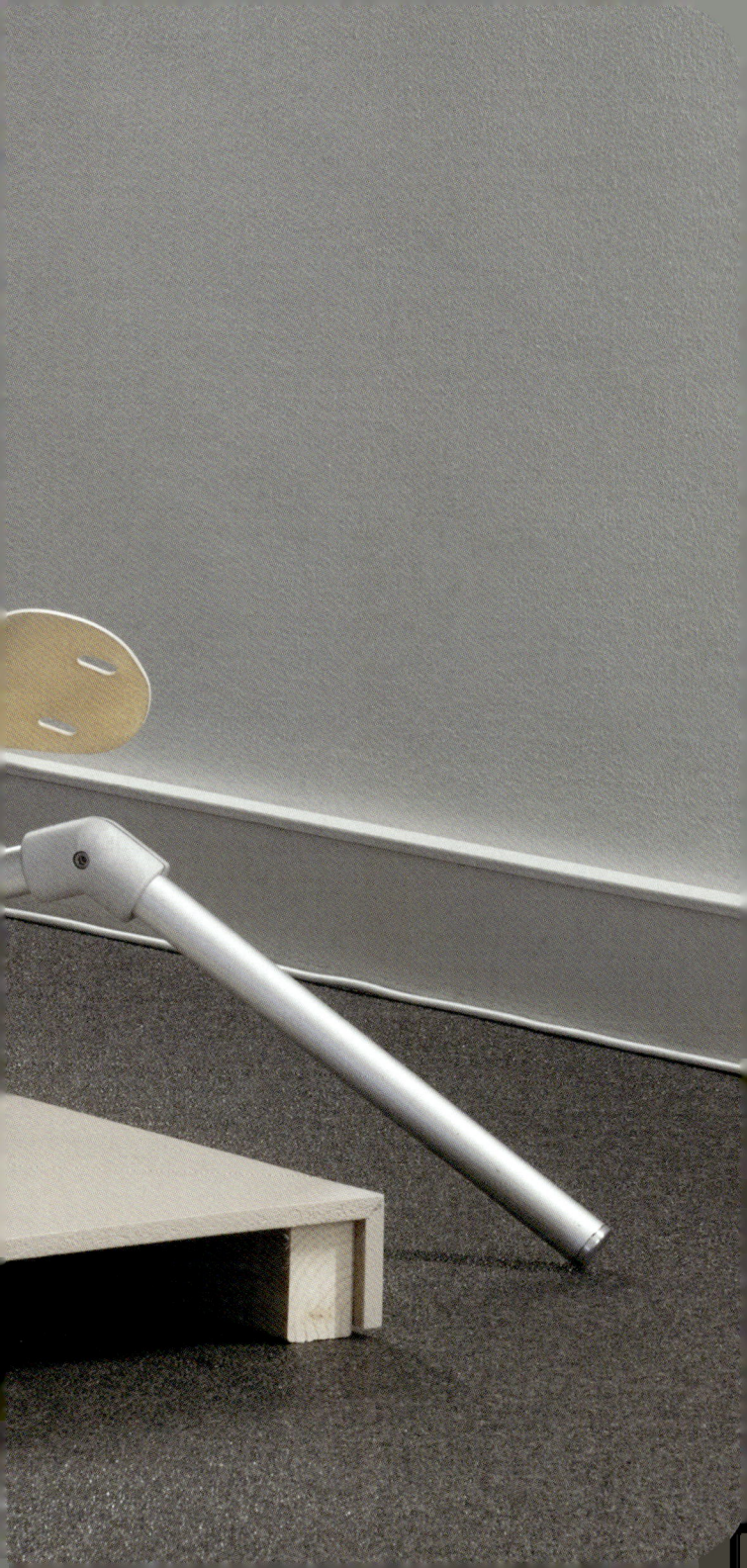

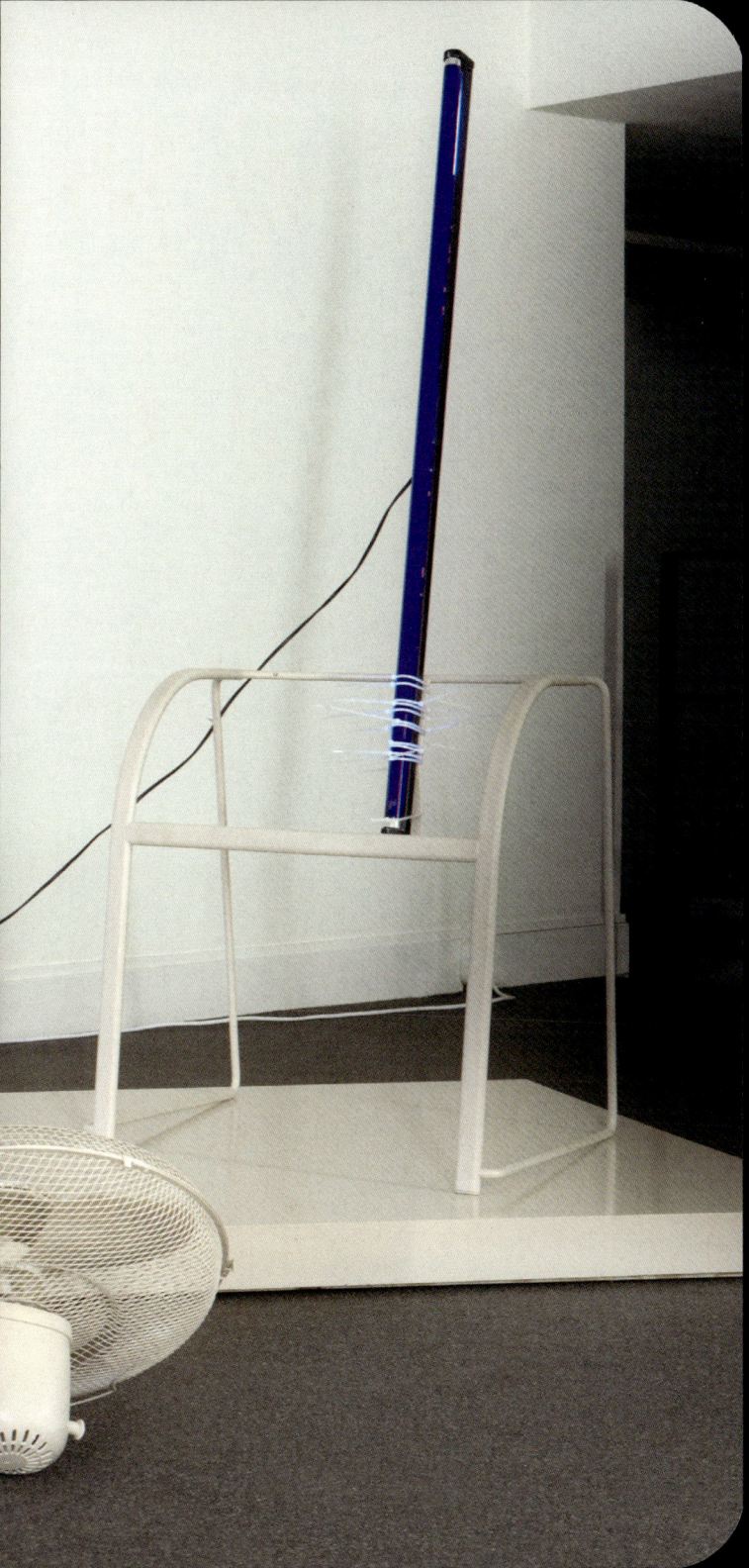

Introduction by Pernilla Ellens

People are nowhere near so fluid

Our best machines are made of sunshine; they are all light and clean because they are nothing but signals, electromagnetic waves, a section of a spectrum, and these machines are eminently portable, mobile – a matter of immense human pain in Detroit and Singapore. People are nowhere near so fluid, being both material and opaque. Cyborgs are ether, quintessence.

> The Cyborg Manifesto, Donna Haraway (1984)

16 December 2017 – 11 March 2018

What would the world be like if humanity were never to leave it, but instead stayed and merged with its materials? This new installation by Janina Frye is situated in the nearby-future, where the evolution of emancipation has taken place. Gender binaries are no longer a topic of discussion and oppositions between subjects have been eliminated. In this time and place, the border between objects and subjects has faded.

In this newly created total installation, concrete blocks, foam rubber, aluminium structures and neon-coloured plastic all bear resemblances to the shapes of a human body. The sculptures move slightly, in an almost pre-reflexive way. They have skins, spines, joints, and are present in the space, having as much agency within our physical world as the traditional subject would. The familiar material structures that we know from hospitals and public

About Janina Frye

transport play a major role in the vernacular of Frye's post-human landscape. The human bodies leave stains and marks on concrete matter; and in its turn, a materiality guides and trains the human body and shapes the way it behaves inside space. Bones, handprints, and phone chargers all leave their traces, and both man-made artefacts as well as physical relics influence the world equally. The border between us and them—the ultimate dismantling of dualism, the perfect peak of dialectics—will be opaque.

Janina Frye (1987, DE)

Janina Frye graduated at the AKV St. Joost, 's-Hertogenbosch in 2014. In a sensitive, but particularly approachable way, she explores the relationship between human, object and material, the atmosphere and the subject, and whether they can be fused in the future. In her work, Frye frequently makes use of philosophical models such as the Actor Network Theory, Post Humanism, New Materiality and Object Orientated Ontology. The underlying aim of Frye's research as an artist, is to break the existing paradigm of the human as the centre of the world. The work of Janina Frye comprises the investigation of what's at the core of objects, consumer products and their functions; while also exploring how to stretch the quality and identity of these things. Frye operates individually as well in collaboration with her partner Gezim Muharemi.

Alicja Melzacka

More or less (than) human: on objects in the practice of Janina Frye

Alicja Melzacka

> *Few things have contributed so greatly to dehumanisation as has the universal human belief that products of the mind are justified only in so far as they exist for men*
>
> Adorno, 1953

Simultaneously to Jane Austen working on her novel *Sense and Sensibility* the literary scene in Britain experienced a florescence of a very different tendency, called by contemporary literary theorists—quite dispassionately— the 'it-narrative'. Characteristic for this storytelling technique was rendering the non-human agent a protagonist of a novel. In this way, the perspective was shifted from the dominant anthropocentrism to the peripheries of objecthood.

In a preposterous manner, this outmoded literary device connects to what is at stake here—the works of Janina Frye. While her practice can be primarily described as object-oriented, Janina does not lose sight of the human perspective, while constantly inventing new ways to challenge it, on both a conceptual and material level. Especially in her recent projects, Janina has set to investigate the limitations and the possible future of humanity in the 'posthuman' era.

More or less (than) human: *on objects in the practice of Janina Frye*

The three subsequent chapters present—in chronological order—the developments within Janina's practice in relation to the posthumanist discourse, in particular to corporeal feminism and object oriented ontology.

ON RELATIONSHIPS

The recent critique of the 'liberal humanist subject' as a 'site of exclusion' has been directed at the processes of becoming-subject, based on the exclusion of those considered to be 'less-than-human', due to—amongst others—gender, sexual orientation or ethnic background (Roffe & Stark, 2015, p. 2). This problem of the uneven subject-object relationship permeating every level of social reality has been addressed by Janina through her artistic practice.

In her video-works from 2014, she set to investigate alternative relationships between humans and objects— outside of the convention of commodity or trophy—following Bill Brown's famous assertion that 'objects and subject animate one another' (2003). Those works show Janina engaging in a series of—rather unexpected—activities directly *with* objects (where the preposition *with* exploits the tension between an instrumental relation and the one based on equity and reciprocity).

A/B

In the video *A/B*, everyday items are turned into abstracted compositional elements in constant re-arrangement. While the objects seem to initiate new links between one another, it is still the arbitrary, maybe even whimsical decision of the artist that governs their distribution in the space. The apparent autonomy of those items, seemingly released from the confinement of utility (and in this very moment, according to the early 'thing theory', crossing the border between 'objects' and 'things'), collides with their unconditional obedience to the 'composer'. The void following their loss of function is immediately filled by a new, aesthetic usage, paradoxically re-objectifying the things, as if within a (mobile) still life.

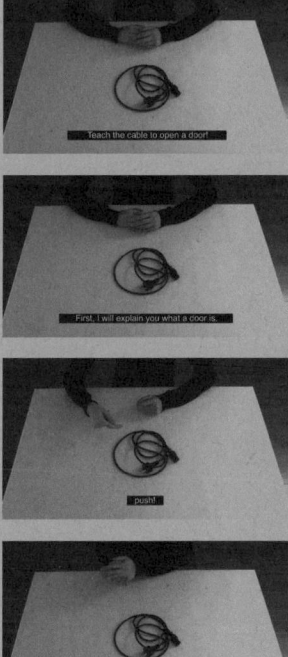

How to teach a cable to open the door

In the 'tutorial' video *How to teach a cable to open the door*, and going a step beyond Baldessari's ambitious exercise in educating a plant (1972), Janina has tried to teach an *inanimate* object a simple operation. The human desire to dominate appears here in the guise of a didactic activity, reduced to a system of simplistic commands, as if taken from the vocabulary of a dog-trainer. Despite the lenient, reassuring character of the teacher, the video is slightly

More or less (than) human: on objects in the practice of Janina Frye

unsettling and exposes that education and indoctrination are often the two sides of the same coin.

The distance between a subject and an object is considerably reduced in *Urlaubsliebe,* an intimate video-work that allows the viewer to observe Janina taking a rickety, foldable table for a stroll through the picturesque town of St Moritz. While the voice-over narrates the origin of the table, the object-to-owner relation seems to transform as the stroll advances. The end of the video finds them both side by side at the lake contemplating the landscape. This scene concludes the 're-singularisation' of an object — a process reversed to those mentioned above in which the table asserts itself for a brief moment as an individual thing. The 'thing' in this instance 'really names less an object than a particular subject-object relation' (Brown, 2001, p. 4).

Urlaubsliebe

However, as disclosed by further analysis, even this seemingly vulnerable work may have darker undertones. Despite being considerably different from the anthropological 'methodological fetishism' as proposed by Arjun Appadurai in the *Social Life of Things* (2001), the discussed approach still maintains the singularity and centrality of a human subject (notably, as opposed to the later works, the artist is physically present). Such perspective makes the understanding of objects as mere mirrors of human nature almost inevitable. Just as the 18th century 'it-tales' can be read as 'allegories of the circulation of women as sexual objects whose market value declines over time' (Blackwell, 2007, p. 13), the interpretation of human-object interactions in the discussed videos as a a metaphor for interpersonal relations, is self-imposed. They seem to mimic the relations within patriarchal societies, where the preferred position of inanimate objects and women alike is that of subordination and subservience. They are projected as eager disciples, obedient followers and, finally, the objects of temporary infatuation—*die Urlaubsliebe.*

ON OBJECT, BODY AND SEXUALITY

An interest in the materiality, or rather physicality of objects is another discernible chapter within Janina's practice and a place where object oriented ontology meets corporeal feminism. This strand of feminism deals in particular with the understanding of a body, challenging its conceptualisation as a fixed object, or 'biological *tabula rasa*' upon which the 'masculine and feminine could be indifferently projected' (Grosz, 1994, p.18).

This idea of a body as a *lacking* counterpart of the mind, rooted within western Cartesian body/mind dualism, has been challenged with the emergence of the notion of *embodied subjectivity,* being in the constant process of renegotiation through biological and social means. In her seminal book *Volatile Bodies* (still firmly anchored in the difference paradigm of the 1990s), Grosz advocated a new understanding of the body as 'a series of processes of becoming, rather than as a fixed state of being' (1994).

By elevating the body from its subservient position, corporeal feminism targets one of the building blocks of western anthropocentrism—a belief in the immaterial consciousness, distinguishing human subjects from other non-human objects. By emphasising the importance of the bodily and material in the constitution of subjectivity, this approach negotiates the common ground between the polarised categories of human and non-human, positioning the body as 'a thing among things' (Merleau-Ponty in: Brown, 2001, p.4).

Corporeal feminist theory devotes a lot of space to discussion on sexuality, which can be seen as an all-encompassing, unifying environment, temporarily redefining the subject-object relations, 'for it seeps across boundaries into areas that are apparently not its own (...) and can draw

More or less (than) human:
on objects in the practice of Janina Frye

Relax and feel well!

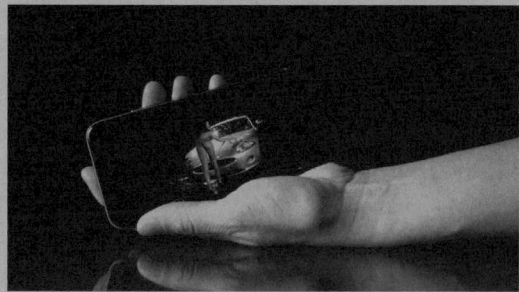

Alicja Melzacka

any object, any fantasy, any number of subjects and combinations of their organs, into its circuits of pleasure' (Grosz, 1994, p. 8). This released sexual potency of inanimate objects has been manifested in several works by Janina and is particularly evident with the multimedia installation *Relax and feel well!* (2016). At first glance, the work appears to revolve around the materiality of a rock, present not only as a 'protagonist' of the video, but also as a pattern imprinted on the bean-bag seats present in the exhibition space. The popular symbolic associations of the stone, in combination with the meditational narration, evokes shallow associations with the westernised image of Zen. Invited by the ethereal voice to sit back and relax, one blissfully follows this benevolent command. A relaxed body, subdued by the power of gravity sinks down into the cushion, entering an ASMR-like trance, almost as if becoming one with the 'stone'. Meanwhile, the stone in the video is being slowly covered with a dripping blue liquid. At some point, it starts receiving a disturbingly sensual massage from a pair of well-kept hands. The built-up tension is released and the trance-like experience brutally disrupted when the voice-over announces: 'imagine whatever you want' and a strongly objectified image of a woman washing a car appears in the place of the stone. This explicit representation of a sexed body stands in strong contrast to the secretive, dormant titillation triggered by the sensual interaction of the human and non-human. Both scenes, however, pertain to the same—though differently apprehended—sexual appeal of objects, thus exposing the concurrent strategies of 'personification of things' and 'reification of people' (Brown, 2001, p. 10). It seems that in a patriarchal society, the degrading model of sexuality represented by the (everything-but-the-) car scene would evoke less controversy than a simple realisation that 'things' too can be arousing.

    A similar positioning of the human body as just another 'thing' occurs in a witty video titled *The innocence of a bottle, a golf club and a leg* (2016), showing the interaction between the three titular bodies, the intentionality of which can be disputed. Does the 'detachment' of a leg from the human body equal the renouncing of any

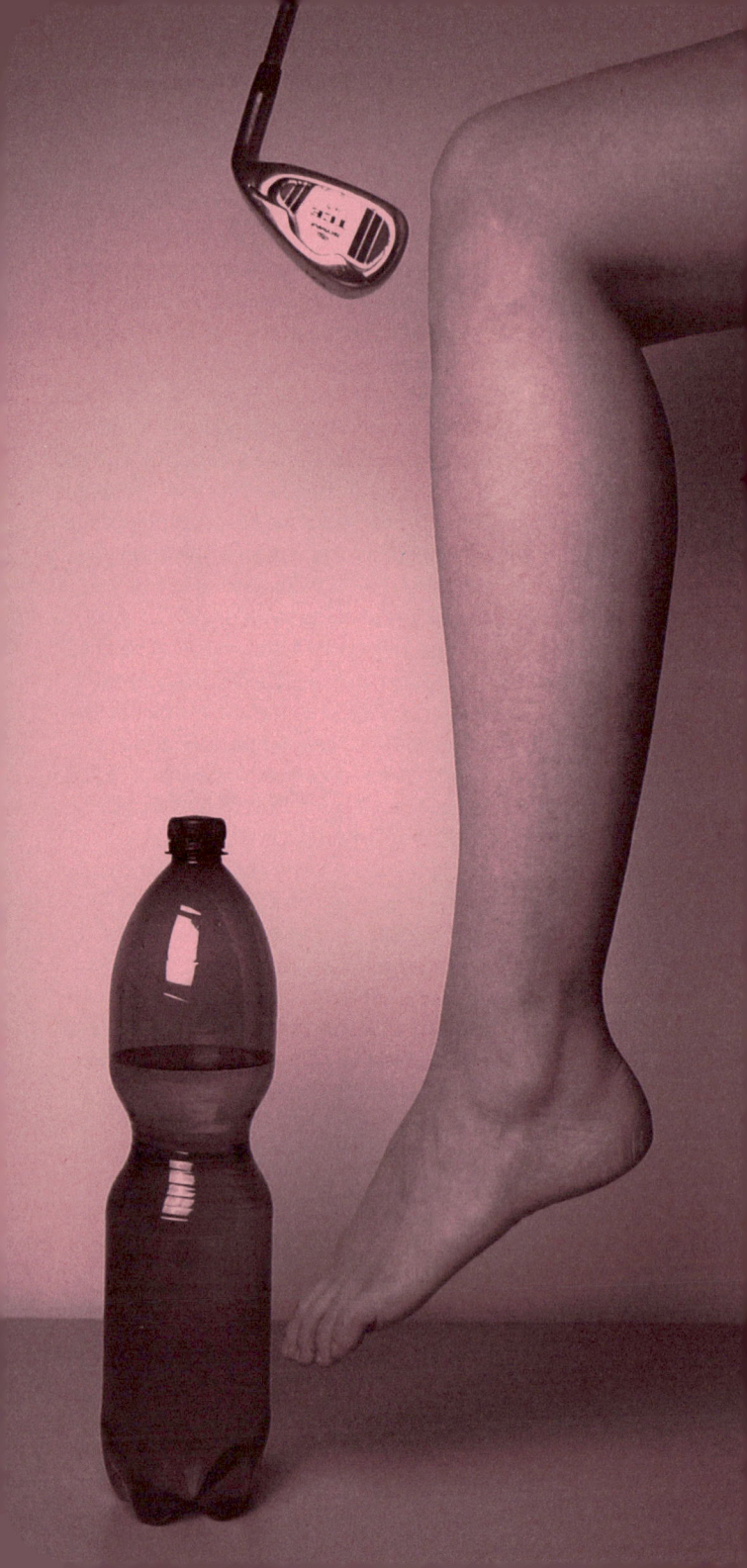

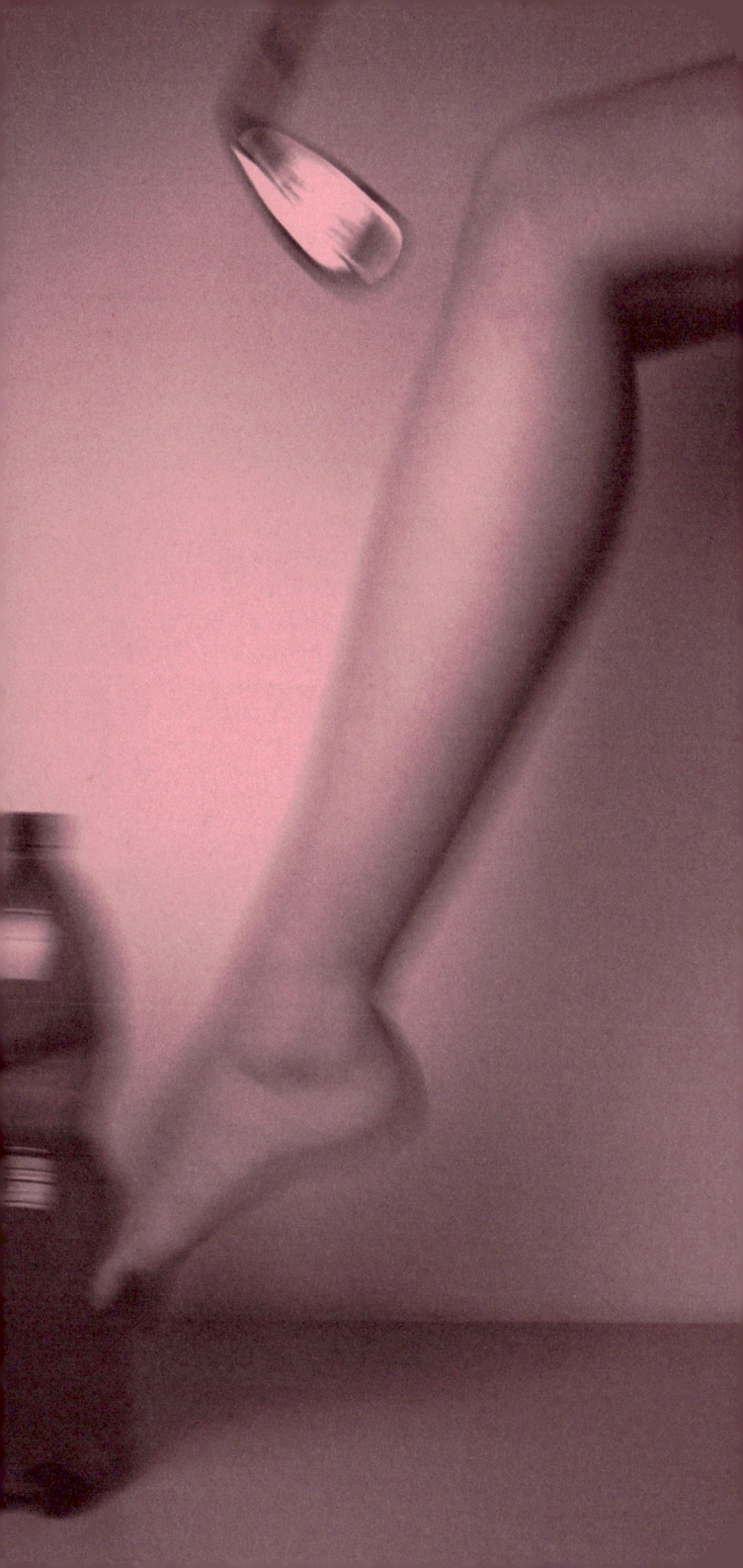

More or less (than) human: on objects in the practice of Janina Frye

responsibility bound to human consciousness? Does any-body in this reaction chain deserve immunity? The abdicated limb itself becomes a tragic character, in which naivety clashes with the necessity to obey the imperative of unconditional reflexes—the symbolic burden of humanity.

The work addresses the supposed vulnerability and innocence of inanimate objects, which we only start to question in the instances of resistentialism—those spiteful little encounters with things which make us trip, bump, slip and lose our temper. Having acknowledged the material autonomy of inanimate objects, in combination with their superior durability in comparison to organic matter, it seems impossible not to respect, or even fear, the non-humans that will inevitably outlast us by hundreds of years. This work, along with a few others of similar thematic content were exhibited during Berlin Art Week in 2016, under the much-telling title —*Better to be an object —tryouts for a better humanity.*

Better to be an object

The problem of a human versus non-human body is probably most imminent in the video-installation *Metamatter* (2016)—a shape-shifting, animated mass, with an uncanny carnal quality. Despite it being an entirely artificial creation, composed of both the corporeal (fabric) and the immaterial (projection), *Metamatter* bears semblance to glistening entrails or a silky-smooth placenta. The work represents the part of Janina's practice focused on material research and the creation of new things rather than their appropriation.

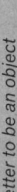
Better to be an object

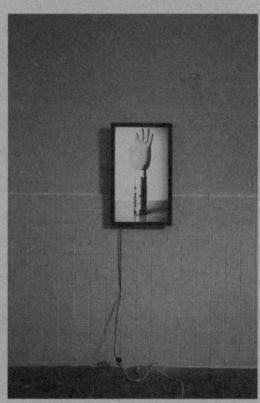

Metamatter can be therefore seen as an attempt at the *embodiment* of a *thing* itself, which Brown poetically described as 'the amorphousness out of which objects are materialized by the (ap)perceiving subject, the anterior physicality of the physical world emerging' (2001, p.5).

THE SHARDS OF MODERNITY AND THE RISE OF A CYBORG

In her recent research, Janina has focused on the phenomenon of de- and re-materialisation of a fragmented human subject through technology, contained in the notion of the 'dividual' (Deleuze, 1992). In contemporary mass society where compulsively producing, consuming and excreting data has become the norm (the process captured by Janina's installation *Born Digital,* 2016, in collaboration with Gezim Muharemi), embodied subjects are reduced to a set of codified parameters. In a dramatic struggle to keep up, fractured bodies have to resort to the very same power of technology that gradually makes them redundant. Today, becoming a 'cyborg' seems the only way to survive.

Donna Haraway's figure of a cyborg was developed in response to her observation of the fading border between humans and non-humans, as 'a fiction mapping our social and bodily reality' (1984, p. 150). This seemingly dystopian vision is more real than we imagine—the *Cyborg Manifesto* dates back to 1984 and since then, our flirt

More or less (than) human: on objects in the practice of Janina Frye

with technology has turned into a permanent betrothal. Contemporary bodies are 'invaded, penetrated and permeated by technologies (...) to the point where the distinction between so-called "original" (technologically uninfected) organisms and extreme new technologies, such as invasive neuro-transplants and infectious nano-robots, has become virtually impossible' (du Preez, 2009).

Metamatter

One of the main lines of inquiry in Janina's recent practice has been the impact of new, replicable technologies on the distinctiveness of the human subject. In the course of their residency in the *Spring House* in 2017, Janina and Gezim experimented with the idea of a professionalised, highly artificial working environment. This resulted in an immersive installation, transforming the office space into a bizarre ecosystem with technology as a second nature.

Contemporary working and living environments are created with an upgraded, more streamlined and efficient humanity in mind. In her most recent project *People are nowhere near so fluid* (2017) Janina reflects on how our bodies can be tailored to suit this hyper-enhanced reality, incorporating to a greater or lesser extent the idea of a cyborg. The way for the project has been paved by a period of material research, during which Janina experimented with a variety of synthetic and compositional materials and their body-like properties. Using plastic, concrete and foam, she developed a series of bizarre 'hybrids' of humans and non-humans, illustrating the transition from anatomic to industrial forms. They incorporate fragments of found

Alicja Melzacka

objects accidentally resembling human anatomy but also elements designed to mimic body parts. Some of these cross-bred objects seem fragile, maybe even mutilated, like prostheses missing their organic counterparts, while others exhibit an almost 'vital' force.

Despite generally operating within the language of industrial design, a few of the objects seem to vaguely echo the fragile constructions of Alexander Calder, or the humanoid sculptures of Henry Moore. They are, however, radically different in their erasure of the humanistic subject and its substitution with a technological, androgynous body. Pushing the imperative of progress to the very extreme has caused its implosion. A cyborg, an 'illegitimate offspring of militarism and patriarchal capitalism' is born amidst the shards of modernity (Haraway, 1984, p. 151).

Just as with the cyborg myth, the works of Janina are 'about transgressed boundaries, potent fusions and dangerous possibilities', resulting from our relationships with technological objects (Haraway, 1984, p. 154). By exposing the oppressive and unsustainable foundations of what we have called the Anthropocene, they force the reconsideration of what it means to be more or less (than) human.

NOTES

Adorno, T. (1988). Valery Proust Museum. In: *Prisms* (p. 173-86). Cambridge: MIT Press.

Brown, B. (2001). Thing Theory. *Critical Inquiry*, vol. 28 (1), p. 1-22.

Brown, B. (2003). *A Sense of Things: The Object Matter of American Literature.* Chicago: University of Chicago Press.

Deleuze, G. (1992). Postscript on the societies of Control. *October,* vol. 59, p. 3-7.

Du Preez, A. (2009). *Gendered Bodies and New Technologies: Rethinking Embodiment in a Cyber-era.* Newcastle upon Tyne: Cambridge Scholars Publishing.

More or less (than) human: on objects in the practice of Janina Frye

Grosz, E. (1994). *Volatile Bodies: toward a corporeal feminism.* Bloomington: Indiana University Press.

Haraway, D. (1991). A Cyborg Manifesto: Science, Technology, and Socialist-Feminism in the Late Twentieth Century (p. 149-81). In: *Simians, Cyborgs and Women: The Reinvention of Nature.* New York: Routledge.

Roffe, J. & Stark, H. (2015) Introduction (p. 1-16). In: J. Roffe & H. Stark (Eds.) *Deleuze and the Non/Human.* Basingstoke & New York: Palgrave Macmillan.

Sense & Sensibility September 17– March 18

145

More Girlfriends!

Curator's note

Because Sense & Sensibility wishes to function as a platform, we invited some other artists besides the main local participants to contribute to the project. We appreciate them for their engaging work, both in ethics and in visual culture. That's why we chose to have snippets of their work exhibited in The Girls' Room.

Meet our newest girlfriends...

Daantje Bons (1987, NL)

Daantje Bons is the photographer connected to the overall Sense & Sensibility project. She has documented all exhibitions and interventions, and has contributed to this, the final publication as well. Her fine art photography can be described as a Gender Playground. In her work, Daantje explores the physical intimacy of both objects and bodily features, in bold colours and playful aesthetics. On the desk and on the bookshelf in The Girls' Room, you can see the pictures *So Hot* and *Features of Femininity*.

www.daantjebons.com

Regeneration (2017)

| Sense & Sensibility | September 17– March 18 |

More Girlfriends!

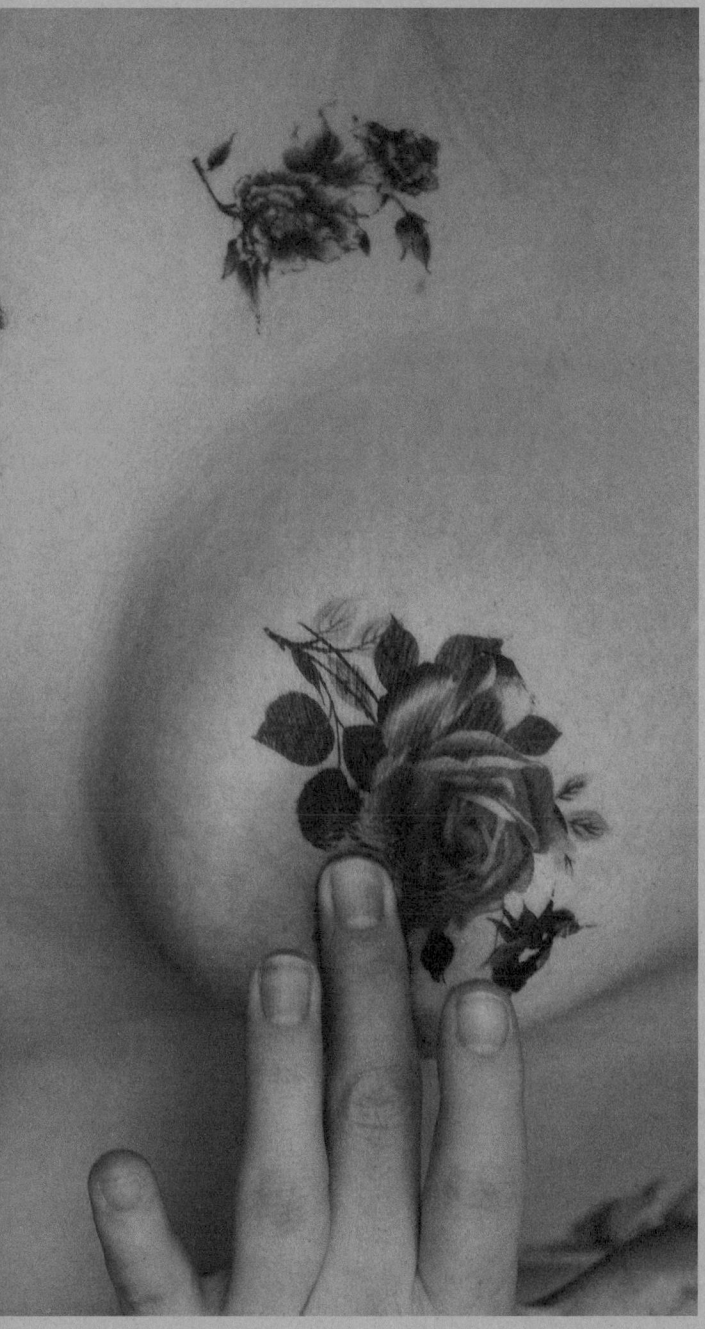

Onomatopee 150 — Nest Project

150 — *Daantje Bons*

So Hot (2015)

More Girlfriends!

Camille Auer

Camille Auer (1984, FIN)

We met the queer trans artist trash academic Camille Auer in Turku, Finland. Camille helped us greatly in defining the premise of the project. If we want to explore power structures based on gender norms, we should therefore not be exclusive but inclusive. Or, as Camille puts it: 'I think it's instrumental to have a wide understanding of girlhood when promoting girl power. Otherwise, it will fall into the category of cis-supremacy instead of the intended gender liberation'. As well as writing, Camille also makes great zines, called *Girldicks*. These 'oestradiol infused transfeminine fits of rage and analysis' are featured in The Girls' Room.

Camille Auer, on transgender rage, in an e-mail conversation with us and in response to Susan Stryker's War With Nature:

'To be trans, indeed sometimes feels like being at odds with nature, but it doesn't make it less real. Where does the validation come from for the natural/artificial dichotomy, anyway? Rage is a part of being human, like any emotion. We don't fight nature necessarily, we make accommodations. I didn't want testosterone in my body, so I cut it off. I don't want to live in a dirt pit, I live in an apartment. We have choice.'

www.camilleauer.com

More Girlfriends!

because i fucking <u>hate</u> trans misogyny and people who spread or protect it.

Ok i know this zine is pretty fucked up and so am i but it never stopped anyone from being right, right?

More Girlfriends!

And it's called girldick which is also fucked up but i like it and i get to say it because it's mine.

But testicles, fuck they're the worst.

Love, Camille

Besides: cisgirls identify by their genitals all the time: PUSSY POWER!

54

Nasty Women

Nasty Women is a global art movement that serves to demonstrate solidarity among artists who identify with being a Nasty Woman in the face of threats to roll back women's rights, individual rights, and abortion rights. With over forty fundraising art exhibitions taking place around the United States and abroad, Nasty Women Exhibitions also serve to support organisations defending these rights as well as being a platform for organising resistance.

Nasty Women flag

Nasty Women is a feminist collective operating from all over the world. We met curator Angel Bellaran in New York, and have been in touch with her since The Girls' Room was still Chelsea Clinton's bedroom. Angel was kind enough to lend us the pink, silk, silkscreened NASTY WOMEN UNITE scarf from her personal collection. The flag, which is now hanging above the bed, was designed and created by San Diego based artist and fellow Nasty Woman, Barbara Smith.

157

More Girlfriends!

| Sense & Sensibility | September 17– March 18 |

159

Theoretical girls

Sense & Sensibility — September 17– March 18

Curator's note

Within Sense and Sensibility, we wish to combine theory and praxis. That's why we asked the participants of the project to invite a writer to contribute a piece to the book regarding the theme. Some pieces were created originally for Sense and Sensibility, in specific relation to the work developed at Onomatopee. Other contributions are texts that the artists found inspirational, engaging and important for their practice and so we have chosen to reprint them in this publication.

Aynouk Tan
Blinded by Fashion – why feminism on a t-shirt is oppression dressed up as politics
(Commissioned)
— on the invite of Pernilla Ellens, relating to
The Girls' Room

Nina Power
The Politics of Pitch
(Commissioned)
— on the invite of Gabriel A. Maher, Roberto Pérez Gayo and Carly Rose Bedford relating to the exhibition "_____" and created as a contextual reflection of their work

Ece Canlı, Luiza Prado de O. Martins
Design and Intersectionality: Material Production of Gender, Race, Class — and Beyond.
(Re-print)
— on the invite of Olle Lundin, relating to the work of *Bureau Just*

Barbara Bolt
Material Thinking and the Agency of Matter
(Re-print)
— on the invite of Janina Frye, relating to
the exhibition *People are nowhere near so fluid*

Aynouk Tan

Blinded by Fashion
–
Why feminism on a T-shirt is oppression dressed up as politics.

Aynouk Tan

It was a somewhat peculiar spectacle when Karl Lagerfeld sent a troop of models marching down the catwalk brandishing placards demanding women's rights. It was for the presentation of his 2015 Chanel spring/summer collection, that the world's highest-paid fashion figures, such as Gisele Bündchen and Cara Delevingne swapped handbags for banners, and pouts for a protest against machoism. The Grand Palais in Paris was transformed in order to match the staged demonstration; marble floors, chandeliers and gold plated wall ornaments were replaced by a street: or rather the decor of a street. The brown-vanilla stone, carving around the windows and the iron curves of the balconies all featured in the trompe l'oeil facades which reached up to the blue sky, visible through the building's glass roof.

This extravaganza *demonstrated*—pun intended—what feminism has recently become: a gordian knot that entangles trend and protest, commodity and politics, popularity and exploitation. This same notion has also been taken up by many celebrities including the likes of Taylor Swift, Beyoncé and Lena Dunham. Hence, feminism

Blinded by fashion - Why Feminism on [...] as politics.

has gained a wide following amongst a significant swathe of young women—judging by their T-shirts at least. Many (online) stores including Dior and Forever 21 have made it possible to express these political views by printing feminist slogans onto textiles. This has led many feminists to question and try to unravel the situation in which feminism finds itself in.

In that sense fashion has become a useful tool for cultural analysis. It represents the economy and ideology, and the social relationships that connect consumers with one another as well as with corporations; and tacitly with the people that produce the clothes. Mundane as it is, or because of its mundanity, fashion represents a system. The question is: can fashion contribute to feminism - thanks to or in spite of, the system which enables it?

Although the social movement in the late '60s has often been used as an argument to emphasise the political value of T-shirts and fashion. The documentary film maker Adam Curtis believes it proves quite the opposite. In his work *The Century of The Self,* Curtis problematises the notion of self-expression and addresses it as one of the pillars of the current economic state:

'The hippie movement started as a rebellion against the state and big business and was aimed at self-expression and self-actualisation. By the end of the century, these new self-actualised individuals became dependent on business for their new identities because business found the way to help them be who they wanted to be. Business turned a threat into the biggest opportunity in history. An old and finite economy based on the static needs of the masses fulfilled by mass produced products was made redundant by an ever changing, and infinite number of individual desires that made infinite economies possible. In this new individualistic society, there is no society really. It's all about the individual and satisfying its desires.'

It must then come as no surprise that it's mainly women who are prone to this idea of 'self-expression' and 'self-actualisation' through appearance. Why are these T-shirts not seen as part of men's collections? Academic Laura Mulvey already formulated the answer in 1975, the year in which she introduced the theory of 'The Male Gaze', a term that still influences feminists to this day. Mulvey explained that the way women are portrayed in visual culture is through the perspective of the heterosexual male—a gaze that has been embodied and internalised by both genders— consequently making the female body a (sexual) object; a spectacle; a body that needs to construct its identity via appearances for the sake of visual pleasure. It therefore nurtures a ubiquitous culture that equates objectification with self-expression.

And so we enter an age in which the person asking for feminist rights must first embody the standards that lay at the foundation of inequality. Or as the feminist writer Roxane Gay so poignantly put forward in an article on the triviality of celebrity feminism: 'Too many people are wilfully ignorant about what the word means and what the movement aims to achieve. But when a pretty young woman has something to say about feminism, all of a sudden, that broad ignorance disappears or is set aside because, at last, we have a more tolerable voice proclaiming the very messages feminism has been trying to impart for so damn long.'

Feminism has oppression ingrained into it, as it deals with who has the right to speak and who is being listened to. When white male fashion designers send out a group of pretty young white models on a catwalk 'demanding women's rights', and obtain a large audience as a consequence: it does exactly what feminism is protesting against. Namely, keeping the gender and racial roles of privilege that the patriarchy and western imperialism has installed on us as the central mechanism of its power.

Who is listening to the voices of those who make our clothes? According to the Clean Clothes Campaign about three quarters of an estimated 75 million international garment workers are women—resulting in about 56 million female garment workers that could be producing your 'feminist' T-shirt under sweatshop conditions.

How do these feminist T-shirts emancipate the position of women of colour? How do they benefit those who are disproportionately vulnerable because they don't have access to the same educational and or class privileges that these "fempreneur" leaders have?

Theoretical girls

Blinded by fashion - Why Feminism on [...] as politics.

Fashion constitutes objectification dressed up as luxury, sexism passing as empowerment, and materialism masquerading as self-care. It is a trompe l'oeil facade, a mundane act that we have become so skilled at performing. It's a veil that has enwrapped us so tightly that we have become blind to what is right in front of us. Fashion is not a T-shirt, it is not a bunch of pretty white women 'demanding women's rights'; fashion is not about ostentatious desires and it is definitely not about feminism.

Fashion is a lens through which we perceive ourselves and others, a social relationship, an ideology. Fashion is a system. As long as we let individual, self-achieving, narcissistic ways of seeing, i.e the capitalist lens, reign our ways of perception, we cannot see that fashion, more than any textile, is a gigantic hub of power structures. As long as we remain blind to that, it's hard to realise that we do not only abide to fashion as system of oppression, we also generate it.

In that respect Lagerfeld did fulfil an important feminist duty. By staging a reality he revealed the absurdity of the mundane; a ubiquitous spectacle that is performed on our streets everyday for us to see. Let that clear vision lead us to the determination that it will be the last 'feminist spectacle' that fashion is allowed to perform. Since a true elimination of oppression is only reached through abolishing hierarchies of the Self - wearing a 'feminist' T-shirt, any T-shirt really, constitutes the exact opposite.

ABOUT AYNOUK TAN

Aynouk Tan observes fashion from an anthropological point of view. As a journalist, curator and art-director she discusses how the clothes we wear constitute our identity and perceptions. In her renowned column 'Fashion according to Aynouk Tan' in the Dutch newspaper NRC Handelsblad she dressed herself weekly in a different outfit to physically address these themes. Tan is also employed as a trend analyst and strategist for different companies and fashion designers. She has curated multiple exhibitions and frequently lectures at (inter)national art academies and universities. As a knowledgeable person on the subject of fashion and feminism, we asked her to write the piece *Blinded by Fashion* especially for this publication.

The Politics of Pitch

Nina Power

Who speaks? Who listens? In a 2012 article entitled 'Why We Prefer Masculine Voices (Even in Women)', the author, Megan Garber, reported that '[s]tudy after study has suggested that low voices, "masculine" voices, are an asset to those seeking leadership roles, in politics and beyond'.[1] Masculine voices time and time again are seen to be more attractive, more competent and most trustworthy. Women who speak in lower tones are also positively read according to this bias, though past a certain depth, lower-voiced women are deemed to be less physically attractive. In the 2012 research project, drawn on by Garber, entitled 'Preference for Leaders with Masculine Voices Holds in the Case of Feminine Leadership Roles' by Rindy C. Anderson and Casey A. Klofstad, they note that, even where hypothetical elections for 'feminine' leadership roles (e.g. in the US context, for Parent Teachers Organisations) were held, that 'men and women preferred female candidates with masculine voices. Likewise, men preferred men with masculine voices. Women, however, did not discriminate between male voices'.[2]

What is it about 'masculine' voices that makes us listen more, regardless of what our own voice might sound like?

1. https://www.theatlantic.com/sexes/archive/2012/12/why-we-prefer-masculine-voices-even-in-women/266350/

2. http://journals.plos.org/plosone/article?id=10.1371/journal.pone.0051216

The Politics of Pitch

Are we inculcated to associate depth of pitch with authority? Over the years, Laurie Anderson has used techniques of 'audio drag' to parody the 'voice of authority' by performing as 'Fenway Bergamot', where sometimes he is a 'blowhard pontificating idiot' and other times he is more melancholy.[3] But we live in a world in which people turn to voice training techniques in order to 'sound like a leader'. Gary Genard, who promotes 'The Genard Method', a kind of 'Performance-Based Public Speaking Training', writes the following: 'One reason my recent client (and many others I've coached) had a voice that sounded too young is that she spoke with too much "head voice." A key distinction you should know about is the dichtomy [sic] between head voice and chest voice: one thin and lightweight, as if it consisted of air; and the other sounding as though it's been left in the basement like an old stuffed chair'.[4] Although Genard claims that his technique applies to men and women alike, he nevertheless makes it clear just how gendered the assumptions he engages with are: '[t]oo "pink" a voice, with work, can suddenly begin to reveal more "burgundy" tones reflecting the maturity and steadfastness of a leader'.

We should sound more like stuffed chairs and red wine, and less like air and young girls. But why should we accept this association of authority with depth and competency? Why should we listen to those with 'masculine' voices and ignore those who speak in higher registers? Behind these strange images of chairs and wine and the association of business with domination, as if we are talking about chimpanzees and banana hoarding, rather than Gary from accounts, lies another image, of the one least listened to – the young girl with a high voice, the polar opposite of 'authority', of 'business', of 'competency'. Supremacy depends upon the hierarchical pitching of men against

3. https://www.musicomh.com/features/interviews/interview-laurie-anderson

4. https://www.genardmethod.com/blog/the-voice-of-authority-how-to-sound-like-a-leader

women, low voices against high, age against youth – and here the frame of the sonic clashes with the realm of the visual, where the image of the 'young girl' is dominant, yet the actual young girl is without any actual power. But could the voice of the young girl become a site of resistance?

In a very recent article, from December 4th, entitled 'Fear of the Female Voice', Sarah Gailey, points out that 'For millennia, Western society has insisted that female voices – just that, our voices – are a threat. We're afraid of wolves, and we're afraid of bears, and we're afraid of women'.[5] One of the difficult things about this claim is that women and girls are hardly ever taught that their voices could be a 'threat'. Rather, we are taught to be afraid, often with good reason. But, precisely because of this paradoxical fear, we are also taught to use our voices to soften life for others, particularly men. The parameters for the range of the female voice are remarkably narrow, highly classed and raced. Women should not dominate conversation (and people are apt to wildly overestimate the percentage of time women speak for, with research showing that men speak 70% of time in mixed gendered groups,[6] and people are recently taking up Dale Spender's work that demonstrates that men think women 'dominate' conversation when they speak for 30% of the time, and that conversation is 'equal' when they speak only 15% of the time). Women shouldn't shout, criticize, scream, demand, laugh too much (and never at men). Stereotypes abound – the overly-loud working class woman, the 'angry black woman', the mad woman, the hysterical woman, the whiney woman, the nag, the shrew, the witch who can control men with her voice, the seductress, and so on. Michelle Obama was criticised for both 'talking like a white girl' *and* for being 'too loud, too angry, or too emasculating'. While we live in

5. https://tor.com/2017/12/04/fear-of-the-female-voice

6. http://www.rolereboot.org/culture-and-politics/details/2015-10-in-mixed-gender-groups-can-you-guess-who-talks-the-most/

a highly visual culture, the voice nevertheless becomes the obscure site of politics – when we talk about the 'voice' of the people, having a voice, or not having one, and so on. Adriana Cavarero's work in *For More Than One Voice: Towards a Philosophy of Vocal Expression* points out that:

> [T]he human condition of uniqueness resounds in the register of the voice. Moreover, the voice shows that this condition is essentially relational. The simple truth of the vocal, announced by voices without even the mediation of articulate speech, communicates the elementary givens of existence: uniqueness, relationality, sexual difference, and age.[7]

Voice is what singularises us, yet at the same time whole swathes of voices are not listened to on the basis precisely of their singularising features. Women's voices have long been positioned as 'too much' or 'not enough' in the public realm. Anne Karpf's work on the human voice notes that:

> Belief in the unsuitability of women's voices for announcing began in the early days of radio, in both the US and Britain. According to the [UK's] Daily Express [in 1928], 'Many hardened listeners-in maintain that… Adam has a more natural broadcasting voice than Eve. Some listeners-in go so far as to say that a woman's voice becomes monotonous after a time, that her high notes are sharp, and resemble the filing of steel, while her low notes often sound like groans.' … The female timbre was singled out for particular opprobrium. The wireless correspondent of the [London] Evening Standard suggested that women's high-pitched voices irritated many listeners, and that they talked too rapidly, over-emphasised unimportant words, or tried to impress listeners by talking beautifully. High voice in women was associated with demureness, and low voice with

---

7. Adriana Cavarero, *For More Than One Voice: Towards a Philosophy of Vocal Expression*, p. 8.

sexuality, so that – in a Catch 22 – the voice that escaped accusations of promiscuity wasn't considered authoritative enough for serious broadcasting.[8]

To return to Cavarero's point regarding the importance of the singularity of the voice, the female voice historically could not win. As Karpf puts it:

> Women were also indicted both for conveying too much personality through their voices ('Critics consider that women have never been able to achieve the "impersonal" touch. When there was triumph or disaster to report, they were apt to reflect it in the tone of their voices') and too little ('For some reason, a man… can express personality better by voice alone than can a woman'). America, too, threw up similar complaints about lack ('Few women have voices with distinct personality,' according to the manager at a Pittsburg radio station) and excess ('Perhaps the best reason suggested for the unpopularity of the woman's voice over the radio is that it usually has too much personality').[9]

This criticism of female voices has not ended – think about the attacks on uptalk (rising terminals) and vocal fry, where young women were particularly criticised for 'sounding dumb'. Hillary Clinton's voice was described as sticking in your ear 'like an ice pick' and accused of 'making angels cry'. Trump mocked her apparent 'robot voice' at one rally.

One of the aspects of the relationship between gender and voice that has most intrigued me over the years is the relationship between what can be pre-recorded and what cannot – that is to say, who gets to be the voice of emergency. Obviously there are many security alerts and messages that can be and are pre-recorded – such as the

---

8. Anne Karpf, *The Human Voice*, 2011.
9. Ibid.

Inspector Sands message – a coded alert that there is a fire somewhere in the station. But what I'm really interested in, is the end of the world announcements, the apocalyptic announcements. The War Book, which was drawn up during the Cold War lays out what the BBC would do in the event of a 'nuclear exchange'. The broadcaster would move to 11 protected bunkers across the UK, called 'Deferred Facilities', which would also house government staff and ministers. The prerecorded war announcement (the 'four-minute warning', named after the approximate length of time from the point at which a Soviet nuclear missile attack against the UK could be confirmed) was read by Radio 4 newsreader Peter Donaldson. It reads:

> This is the Wartime Broadcasting Service. This country has been attacked with nuclear weapons. Communications have been severely disrupted, and the number of casualties and the extent of the damage are not yet known. We shall bring you further information as soon as possible. Meanwhile, stay tuned to this wavelength, stay calm and stay in your own homes.

A 1963 government publication states that in Scotland, people would be informed by 'oral or whistle message' rather than sirens or church bells as used elsewhere in the UK that fallout was expected in one hour. It was clear, though, that the voice had to be well-known and reassuring. As Harold Greenwood from the Ministry of Posts and Telecommunications put it in a 1974 letter: 'an unfamiliar voice' would lead listeners to conclude that 'perhaps after all the BBC has been obliterated'.

The Wartime Broadcasting Service was decommissioned in 1992, and it is not clear what exactly has replaced it. In an article entitled 'The Use of Male or Female Voices in Warnings Systems: A Question of Acoustics' published in Noise & Health: *A Bimonthly Inter-disciplinary International Journal* by Edworthy, Hellier and Rivers from 2003, the authors write: 'Speech warnings and communications systems are increasingly used in noisy, high workload environments. An important decision in the development of such systems is the choice of a male or female speaker'.[10] The paper goes on to argue that, despite the many misconceptions on the topic, 'the choice of the speaker should depend on the overlap of noise and speech spectra'. 'Female voices,' they continue, 'do however appear to have an advantage in that they can portray a greater range of urgencies because of their usually higher pitch and pitch range'.

Cliffor Nass, author of *Wired for Speech*, suggests that people tend to perceive female voices as helping us solve our problems by ourselves, while they view male voices as authority figures who tell us the answers to our problems – the lady vanishes! This might help to explain the upsetting and everyday experience of 'Bropropriating' – taking a woman's idea and taking credit for it.

Why are so many personal assistance and public voices female? Earlier this year, Ikea asked 12,000 people whether they wanted their AI to have a gender in the first place. 44% said they would prefer it to be neutral, though this broke down into 36% of men and 62% of women. Are women sick of Siri et al's sexist continuum with ideas of the female secretary and female subservience?

I want to finish by moving away a little bit from thinking about intimate technologies towards thinking of the way in which voices come to dominate us in the city, and how some ways of talking are being closed-off or diminished. In 2015, it was reported that of the 75% of UK adults who own a smartphone, a quarter never use it for calls. Three years prior, 96% of users were making at least one standard voice call a week. Of course, people are communicating in other ways – through instant messaging, text messaging, WhatsApp, etc. – talking without speaking. People have described this as 'the luxury of asynchronous communication', where we no longer have to respond

10. https://www.ncbi.nlm.nih.gov/pubmed/14965452

in the moment. Other US research suggest that 39% of so-called Millennials interact more with their smartphones than they do with their significant others, parents, friends, children or co-workers. One of the many questions these tendencies raise is – what happens to voices in the city when we no longer use our own? When we are surrounded by voices we do not choose to hear – on transport, on Tannoys, in supermarkets – what room is there left for the singularity of our own vocal being in the world?

ABOUT NINA POWER

Nina Power is a tutor on the Critical Writing in Art & Design programme in the School of Arts & Humanities at the Royal College of Art, London. Nina received her PhD in Philosophy from Middlesex University on the topic of Humanism and Anti-Humanism in Post-War French Philosophy. She is the author of *One-Dimensional Woman* (Zer0, 2009) and Das kollektive politische Subjekt – Aufsätze zur kritischen Philosophie (Laika, 2015), a collection of her philosophical writings (translated into German). Nina's current interests include empathy, psychoanalysis, sex/gender, theories of collectivity, art & activism, decapitalism, social reproduction and ideas of justice. She has written the piece *The Politics of Pitch* especially for this publication.

Sense & Sensibility — September 17– March 18

Ece Canlı & Luiza Prado de O. Martins

> This text has been transcribed from the opening speech of the Intersectional Perspectives on Design, Politics and Power Symposium, which took place on 14 and 15 November 2016 in Malmö, Sweden. It has been lightly edited for clarity and cohesion.

Design and Intersectionality: Material Production of Gender, Race, Class – and Beyond.

Ece Canlı & Luiza Prado de O. Martins

As you must have been following, in the recent years, the world has been facing incredible and devastating incidents; some that we have been watching online, some that we have witnessed directly, some that we have been reacting through social media to, like protesting on the streets or so on. To remember some featured examples: public revolts and social movements that spread from the Middle East to Latin America, the nuclear disaster in Fukushima, war in Syria and the refugee "crisis" blasted in Europe, the rise of extreme right wing parties and dictator-like governments in various states, public massacres by

Design and Intersectionality: Material [...] and Beyond.

radical groups in several countries, the massacre of the Latinx LGBTQI+ community in Orlando, Brexit, and the victory of Donald Trump, just a few days ago... Many people have been reacting to these incidents, every time with rage and despair, yet describing each moment as a "state of exception" or "emergency", crying out for a miraculous change and collective action. However, such events represent just a very small visible portion of the overall picture of the ongoing effects of power, coloniality, modernity and capitalism; and misery, exclusion, subjugation, poverty and death, which are the everyday reality for many people in the world, rather than states of exception.

For decades, activists and scholars have discussed such forms of injustice and oppression from various viewpoints. Feminist movements in particular have been prominent in terms of bringing systematic inequality, violence and oppression towards women into view. By the early 1980s, it was not only gender activism that received significant recognition, but also the struggles of people of colour had become fairly visible and compelling, both on the streets and in academia. However, while gender studies were still focusing on the experiences of white women, race studies were revolving largely around the experiences of black men (McCall, 2005). There was no space for women of colour, suffering not only from gender discrimination and sexism, but also from racism; and consequently classism. While the early feminist scholars of colour called this gender-race-class driven suffering "triple oppression" (Yuval-Davis & Anthias,1983), other feminists includingGloria Anzaldúa, Cherríe Moraga, Angela Davis, Chandra Mohanty, Nira Yuval-Davis, amongst others, argued that these three things should not be regarded as mutually exclusive or separate identity categories, but intertwined axes of social power. In other words, oppression based on one's gender, race and class, cannot be tackled without understanding the greater matrix of power relations working on the bodies concertedly. Kimberlé Crenshaw (1989) later coined the term "intersectionality" to explain this phenomenon, in which different facets of oppression intersect and interact, defining one's social position. These

Ece Canli &
Luiza Prado de O. Martins

axes vary from gender, race and class to sexuality, skin-colour, ethnicity, nation, state, culture, ability, age, origin, wealth, religion, stage of social development etc. (Lutz, 2002; Yuval-Davis, 2006: 202). The objective of taking these distinct forms of oppression into account is not to compare them, which would be a useless endeavour. Rather, acknowledging the complexity of oppression and the multiple shapes it might assume is a helpful strategy in understanding its mechanisms. Intersectionality is not a discipline by itself; rather, it is considered a meta-theory (Davis, 2002), a metaphor (Crenshaw, 1989), a theoretical stance or an approach that has already had a profound influence in a wide range of fields. Accordingly, in this symposium, we would like to permeate the potentiality of intersectionality into design, as we think that it could be a useful method for understanding design's contribution to reproduction of such identity categories, hegemonic power and forms of oppression. And through this, we would like to expand the question and discuss the politics and political agency of design.

Our claim as design researchers is that design, as a practice and discipline, is not exempt from these incidents and effects, but directly involved with or at the back of them. Most people/designers assume that such worldly issues such as social differentiation and unequal distribution of resources are of interest to legislative, institutional and financial practices, and mainly state politics. However, if we do some "detective work" in the words of political scientist Langdon Winner (1980), we can see how the system of inclusion/exclusion, privilege/oppression and social segregation is reproduced through and manifested in designed artefacts, spaces, sites and technologies. Design is a discipline deeply entangled in the dynamics of inequality. It enacts and enforces them; it is both a producer of these mechanisms, and is informed by them. Assuming that issues of inequality and oppression are a matter of institutional politics, and downplaying design's role in the maintenance of these systems is a dangerous path to follow, yet one that the design discipline seems all too eager to walk. It is a path that tends to silence dissenting

Design and Intersectionality: Material [...] and Beyond.

narratives, because it assumes that design (and, by extension, the designer) cannot be anything but fundamentally well intentioned. As such, any criticism is perceived with suspicion, if not downright hostility. Why question something that is inherently good? Why so much skepticism, even towards fields within design that are supposed to concern themselves with social issues?

In such an environment, critical engagements with the insidious mechanisms that inform the process of designing are frequently stifled: if they are even managed to be discussed at all. This unwillingness to examine design's role in the maintenance of oppression only reinforces the need for a profound critical engagement with intersectionality. As a discipline, design is terribly late to a discussion that has been happening within other fields in the Humanities for decades now, and we have a great amount of work to do in order to overcome this. To paraphrase Ivan Illich: to hell with good intentions! It is urgent that we inquire about design's role in sustaining heteronormativity, sexism, racism, xenophobia, and classism. It is essential, particularly given recent events, that we examine the ways in which design contributes to the continuation of the project of coloniality and white supremacy. Borrowing the words of Argentine semiotician Walter Mignolo (2011), "a radical epistemological shift is needed, one that will change not only the content, but the very terms of the conversation." This is no easy task, of course; it is a collective undertaking, one that requires that we challenge each other, that we reflect upon our own modes of operating in the field, and that we look beyond the surface of the obvious.

Let us look into the gentrified and privatised public spaces that push the lower-class to the outskirts of the cities; to the high security checkpoints at the borders and airports that legalise/illegalise bodies with "wrong"/"right" papers; the everyday gendered goods that underpin the representation of heteronormativity and performativity of feminine/masculine and female/male dichotomies; the gender segregated public bathrooms that enforce binary perceptions of gender and silence queer and trans identities...

Such examples, as we call "material co-enactments of design and politics", regulate and manipulate the body's abilities, movements, inhabitations and life conditions in various ways, while segregating society through race, ethnicity, social and legal status, gender, sexuality, nationality and so on.

Apart from such evident examples of artefacts, spaces and technologies, talking about intersectionality in the context of design also requires us to see the greater ecology of material power. For instance, we believe that it is not possible to talk about design and its relation to politics and power without thinking of its direct involvement in neoliberal capitalist economy, and as being the backbone of the mechanisms of production and consumption. In parallel, the sustainment of this economy is one of the most central foci of intersectional critique, as the global labour market is the first hand regulator of the gendered, racialised and impoverished bodies (Mohanty, 2003, Salem, 2016). We can open this argument by stressing that today most of the technological gadgets we depend on (say, our smart phones and laptops), the garments we dress in, the cosmetics we use, toys, electronic appliances, plastic goods, textiles etc. are substantially manufactured in the Third World/Global South from the Far East to Latin America by mostly under age women of colour—the poorest and the most precarious bodies in all the world. Chandra T. Mohanty (2003: 514) states that "women do two thirds of the world's work and earn less than one-tenth of its income" under dehumanising working conditions; without insurance, security, sufficient sleep, nutrition and future. In their article about global assembly lines, Barbara Ehrenreich and Annette Fuentes (1981: 94-95) stress that "eighty to ninety percent of the low-skilled assembly jobs that go to the Third World are performed by women" in the service of "foreign–dominated industrialisation." They describe these young poor women of colour as "the world's new industrial proletariat" (ibid.). Considering that all the products and services produced by these exploited bodies are "design", one can then say that the

Design and Intersectionality: Material [...] and Beyond.

unremitting machine of design and production are at the center of the gender-race-class persecution.

Taking these examples and concerns into account, as the Decolonising Design Group, we initiated this symposium to stir discussions about intersectionality, and to scrutinise the categories and axes of power that design is implicated in. We are aware that in recent decades, many designers and design researchers have been directing their paths towards disadvantaged and marginalised groups or engaging themselves with community projects to "empower people". These designers have been increasingly discussing the notion of "politics" and its relation to design. Yet, they either consider problems too complicated and ignore them because they think that design is not in charge of those problems; or they try to "solve" things that are beyond the capability/limits of design practice. These very disadvantages are historically, practically and epistemologically deployed; how design/material configurations are the first hand actors in this deployment is yet to be articulated. This is sometimes due to the difficulties involved in such possible discourses, and sometimes due to a lack of understanding and self-reflection.

With this symposium, we attempt to initiate a space for discussing the concept of intersectionality from the viewpoint of design, designing in particular and materiality in general. We ask — how does design and designing participate and reinforce power structures in an intersectional way, through and across race, gender and class — and other identity categories in the matrix of power? How can design and designing offer novel methods to understand the manner in which power operates in intersectional ways? And possibly, how can design and designing propose ways of intervening in such complex and intersectional power relations?

During these two days, we will approach these — and other questions related to intersectionality — through a wide spectrum of topics and angles. In so doing, we hope to advance debates on the materialisation of power through design, to stimulate and foster intersectional and critical discourse, and to contribute to the consolidation of an urgent shift in how we understand, do, and approach design research and praxis.

REFERENCES

Anthias, Floya, and Nira Yuval-Davis. 1983. "Contextualizing Feminism: Gender, Ethnic and Class Divisions." *Feminist Review* 15: 62–75

Crenshaw, Kimberlé. 1989. "Demarginalizing the Intersection of Race and Sex: A Black Feminist Critique of Antidiscrimination Doctrine, Feminist Theory and Antiracist Politics." *University of Chicago Legal Forum (PhilPapers)* 140: 139-167

Davis, Kathy. 2002. "Intersectionality as Buzzword: A Sociology of Science Perspective on What Makes a Feminist Theory Successful." *Feminist Theory* 9 (1): 67–85

Ehrenreich, Barbara, and Annette Fuentes. 1981. "Life on the Global Assembly Line." *Ms. Magazine* 9 (7): 52-59

Lutz, Hemla. 2002. "Intersectional Analysis: A Way Out of Multiple Dilemmas?" Paper presented at the International Sociological Association Conference, Brisbane, Australia, July 7-13

McCall, Leslie. 2005. "The Complexity of Intersectionality." *Journal of Women in Culture and Society* 30 (3): 1771-1800

Mignolo, Walter D. 2011. *The Darker Side of Western Modernity: Global Futures, Decolonial Options*. Durham: Duke University Press

Mohanty, Chandra T. 2003. "'Under Western Eyes' Revisited: Feminist Solidarity through Anticapitalist Struggles." *Signs* 28 (2): 499-535

Salem, Sara. 2016. "Intersectionality and Its Discontents: Intersectionality as Traveling Theory." *European Journal of Women's Studies:* 1-16

Design and Intersectionality: Material [...] and Beyond.

Winner, Langdon. 1980. "Do Artifacts Have Politics?" *Daedalus* 109 (1): 121-136 Yuval-Davis, Nira. 2006. "Intersectionality and Feminist Politics." *European Journal of Women's Studies* 13 (3): 193-209

ABOUT THE AUTHORS

Ece Canlı is a design researcher and performance artist, born in Turkey and based in Porto, Portugal. She is currently a PhD candidate in the Design program at University of Porto, where she investigates the intersection between queer theory and design practice by looking at materiality of body politics. Her tools of investigation include artefacts, texts, sound and voice. She is one of the founding members of Decolonising Design Group.

Luiza Prado de O. Martins is a design researcher in gender studies, and is currently a PhD Candidate at the Universität der Künste Berlin. She holds a BA in Graphic Design from PUC-Rio, (Rio de Janeiro, Brazil), and an MA in Digital Media from the Hochschule für Künste Bremen (Germany). Her research investigates the relationship between contraceptive technologies and the establishment of colonial gender systems.

Material Thinking and the Agency of Matter

Barbara Bolt

In the theory of means and ends that dominates our contemporary understanding of the artistic process, we tend to focus on the instrumental use of tools and materials to make an artwork. According to this view, the artist and craftsperson is the one who exercises mastery over his/her tools and materials to produce an artwork. In harnessing means to ends, the artist justifiably can sign her/his name as the one who has made or caused a work of art to come into being.

In his essay 'The question concerning technology' (1977), Heidegger lays the foundations for a different relation to technology and to matter, a way of thinking that helps us reconsider the artistic relation in a post human age. Where we have come to accept the view that humans use tools, materials and methods to achieve an artistic end, Heidegger makes the claim that four ways of being responsible let art emerge. In the example of the making of the silver chalice, Heidegger identifies the responsible elements involved in the process as matter, aspect and circumscribing bounds

Material Thinking and the Agency of Matter

(Heidegger 1977: 6). Together with the artist, these ways of being responsible do not make an artwork, since art, is not concerned with making. Rather, they enable or bring-forth something into appearance.

In his discussion of indebtedness and responsibility and later in his elaboration of *techne* as *poiesis*, Heidegger suggests a different relationship or engagement than that of instrumentality. For Heidegger it is *techne*, through art and handcraft that humans participate in conjunctions with other contributing elements in the emergence of art. In Heidegger's use of the term "concernful dealings", there is the suggestion that the relationship between humans and the ready-to-hand involves an ethics other than the ethics of mastery.

Heidegger's discussion of responsibility and indebtedness provide us with quite a different way to think about artistic practice. In the place of an instrumentalist understanding of our tools and material, this mode of thinking suggests that in the artistic process, objects have agency and it is through the establishing conjunctions with other contributing elements in the art that humans are co-responsible for letting art emerge.

When Heidegger was writing his 'Technology' essay between 1949 and 1954, the possibility of attributing agency to objects was, at least in the west, largely unthought. However in a post-human context the work of contemporary philosophers of science, Bruno Latour and Donna Haraway, posit the argument that "objects" are actors with agency. This emphatic assertion enables us to revisit the relationship between the artist, the tools of production and the materials of production and recast this relationship.

Haraway introduces the 'power-charged social relation of "conversation"' (Haraway 1991: 198). In this conversation, she contends, the world is not raw material for use by humans (Haraway 1991: 198). Haraway argues that the agency of the world is central for revisioning the world and refiguring a "different" politics of practice whereby the tools of practice are not used merely used to achieve an

Barbara Bolt

end and matter is no longer a resource to be used by humans in order to make an artwork. The central term in Haraway's elaboration is the material-semiotic actor. This actor may be human or non-human, machine or non-machine.[1] What is critical to her position is that the material-semiotic actor actively contributes to the production. Thus an "object of knowledge" is no longer a resource, ground, matrix, object, material or instrument to be used by humans as a means to an end. Rather an object of knowledge is an 'active, meaning-generating axis of the apparatus of bodily production' (Haraway 1991: 200).

Haraway's notion of the material-semiotic actor grew out of her engagement with writer Katie King's "apparatus of literary production". In King's schema, the apparatus of literary production is the matrix that spawns "literature". Literature emerges at the intersection of art, business and technology (Haraway 1991: 200). In this ensemble, language is as much an actor as the author. As Haraway sees it:

> King's objects called "poems"... are sites of literary production where language also is an actor independent of intentions and authors, bodies as objects of knowledge are material-semiotic generative nodes. Their boundaries materialize in social interaction. (Haraway 1991: 200-201)

In this way, Haraway attends to the relations and forces that take place within the very process or tissue of making.

---

1. See also Bruno Latour's elaboration of objects as actors, particularly his article 'Mixing Humans and Nonhumans Together: the Sociology of a Door Stopper' (1998). In his theorising, Latour conceives of objects as lieutenants who have been delegated to carry out particular functions. Thus he argues that what defines our social relations is in large measure prescribed back to us by non-humans. In this, he continues, 'knowledge, morality, craft, force, sociability are not properties of humans but of humans accompanied by their retinue of delegated characters' (Latour 1988:301).

Material Thinking and the Agency of Matter

As she makes clear, these are some of the 'lively languages that actively intertwine in the production of literary value' (Haraway 1991: 210).

In Haraway's theorisation of the material-semiotic actor— with its emphasis on language as an actor independent of intentions, and bodies as material-semiotic generative nodes— enables us to rethink the artistic relation. In this encounter, the human is no longer outside of the assemblage directing the proceedings. The human being becomes just one material-semiotic actor engaged in complex conversation with other players.

The dialogical and emergent nature of literary production resonates with Edward Sampson's (1999) notion of the "acting ensemble". For him, the acting ensemble presents a dialogical construct that takes into account the emergent quality of creative practice. He would argue that creativity, like intelligence, is the property of the acting ensemble, not the individual. The acting ensemble takes in the totality of the acting environment. We are, Sampson proposes, 'woven together with context'. He speaks of 'embodied interactive emergence', arguing that the acting ensemble is characterised by its emergent property. This removes the focus from the acting individual and places it in the relations between actors. In this shift from the individual artist to the relations between the individual body, the social body and the material conditions of making (say a painting), the actors can include paint, the canvas, type of support, the weather, the

2. Haraway distinguishes between actors and actants. Actors have character, whilst actants operate at the level of function (Haraway 1992:331). In that sense, it may be suggested that actors with their own particularities contribute to actants, which are structured according to what they do. Thus humans and non-humans become part of the 'functional collective that makes up an actant' (Haraway 1992:331). In Heidegger's example, silver smithing could be seen to be the actant bringing together a collective of actors including the silver, equipment, chemicals and the artist(s) in productivity.

Barbara Bolt

wind and gravity as well as discursive knowledges.[2] Brian Massumi's description of the relation between the woodworker, the wood and the plane, supports this focus on the agency of the matter. In this relation the signs in the wood are not passive, even if their action is slower and their force less active than the tool or the human. In the encounter, which Brian Massumi defines as the "hand-to-hand combat of energies" we can no longer focus on form. Rather what emerges:

> . . . is a dynamism, composed of a number of interacting vectors. The kind of "unity" it has in no way vitiates that multiplicity—it is precisely an interaction between a multiplicity of terms, an interrelation of relations; an integration of disparate elements. (Massumi 1992:14)

This focus on the acting ensemble rather than the artist as the locus of art enables us to come closer to an understanding of the dynamism of material practice and to the radicality offered by the notion of material thinking. In this dynamism, the outcome cannot be known in advance. Thus although we may have some awareness of the potential of a tool or a piece of wood—for example, through previous dealings with wood and tools—every new situation brings about a different constellation of forces and speeds. The wood may be a bit harder, the tool sharper or blunter and our own energies more or less focussed. Thus our relation to technical things is inevitably characterised by a play between the understandings that we bring to the situation and the intelligence of our tools and materials. This relation is not a relation of mastery but one of co-emergence.

I would like to argue that contemporary artists often become so pre-occupied with intentionality, meaning and making an artwork, they tend to reduce their materials and tools to a means to an end. In this paper I have presented a challenge to this way of thinking and acting. I have proposed that creative practice can be conceived of as a performance in which linkages are constantly being made

Material Thinking and the Agency of Matter

and remade. Whilst each actor has the same praxiological status, each has its own character and contribution to make as part of the work of art.

REFERENCES

Haraway, D. (1991) *Simions, Cyborgs and Women*, New York: Free Association Books.

Haraway, D. (1992) 'The Promises of Monsters: A Regenerative Politics for Inappropriate/d Others', in L. Grossberg. C. Nelson and P.A. Treichler, *Cultural Studies*, New York: Routledge: 295-337.

Heidegger, M. (1977) *The Question Concerning Technology and Other Essays*, trans. W. Lovitt, New York: Garland.

Massumi, B. (1992) *A User's Guide to Capitalism and Schizophrenia: Deviations from Deleuze and Guattari*, Cambridge: MIT Press.

Sampson, E.E. (1999) 'To Think Differently: The Acting Ensemble: A New Unit for Psychological Inquiry', unpublished conference paper presented at the Millenium World Conference in Critical Psychology, University of Western Sydney, April 1999.

ABOUT BARBARA BOLT

Barbara Bolt is a practising artist and art theorist who lectures at the Victorian College of Arts and Melbourne Conservatorium of Music at the University of Melbourne. Her practice investigates the material possibilities of painting in a digital age and the relationship between painting and light. Her publications include two monographs Art Beyond Representation: The Performative Power of the Image (2004) and Heidegger Reframed: Interpreting Key Thinkers for the Arts (2011). She maintains a strong dialogue between practice and theory. The piece *Material Thinking and the Agency of Matter* first appeared in *Studies in Material Thinking* Vol. 1, No. 1 (April 2007), AUT University.

COLOPHON

Onomatopee 150
Sense & Sensibility: what a girl wants, what a girl needs

Published in relation to
the NEST 2017 project
at Onomatopee, Eindhoven

ISBN: 9-789-491-677854

Contributing artists: Camille Auer, Daantje Bons, Janina Frye, Victoria Ledig, Olle Lundin, Gabriel A. Maher with Roberto Pérez de Gayo & Carly Rose Bedford, Mandy Roos, Barbara Smith for Nasty Women

Contributing authors: Barbara Bolt, Charlotte van Buylaere, Ece Canlı and Luiza Prado de O. Martins, Pernilla Ellens, Alicja Melzacka, Nina Power, Aynouk Tan

Photography: Daantje Bons, unless noted otherwise
(see table of images)
Final editing: Pernilla Ellens
Proofreading: Josh Plough & Alexandra Fraser
Graphic design: Virginie Gauthier

Printing and lithography:
Unicum by Gianotten, Tilburg

Special thanks to:
Freek Lomme, Guus van der Velden, Lucy Rose Nixon, Mook Attanath, Erik Muijsenberg, Glenn Peeters, Isabel Mager, Sara Kaiser, Gezim Muharemi, Roel Neuraij, Lara Konrad, Angel Bellaran

Edition: 1200

Made possible by:
Stichting Cultuur Eindhoven,
The Mondrian Fund
The Province of Brabant

Onomatopee and authors © 2018

www.onomatopee.net
Send fanmail to
pernilla@onomatopee.net

All rights reserved. No part of this publication may be reproduced, stored in a retrieval system, or transmitted in any form or by any means, electronic, mechanical, photocopied, recorded or otherwise, without the prior written permission from the authors and the publisher.

About NEST:
NEST is an ongoing series at Onomatopee in which four local emerging visual makers are given the platform to create new work, while also being able to explore, deepen and reflect upon their practice in connection to the other participants and contributing writers. Sense & Sensibility is the NEST 2017 project, with its four chosen participants being Mandy Roos, Gabriel A. Maher, Olle Lundin, and Janina Frye.

TABLE OF IMAGES

All photography by Daantje Bons, except for:

p. 13: still from movie
Bring it on (2000)
p. 14: still from movie
But I'm a cheerleader (1999)
p. 14: still from movie
Hairspray (1962)
p. 15: Lucy Rose Nixon
p. 16: Mook Attanath
p. 40: Mandy Roos
p. 45: Glenn Peeters
p. 47: Mandy Roos
p. 48: Glenn Peeters

p. 50–53: Kyle Tryhorn
p. 55: Kyle Tryhorn
p. 56: Lucy Rose Nixon
p. 64: Kyle Tryhorn
p. 105: Charlotte van Buylaere
p. 114–118: Noortje Knulst
p. 120–128: Noortje Knulst
p. 131–142: Janina Frye
p. 153–157: Lucy Rose Nixon